THE SOUL
TELLS A STORY

Engaging Creativity with
Spirituality in the Writing Life

VINITA HAMPTON WRIGHT

IVP

InterVarsity Press
Downers Grove, Illinois

InterVarsity Press
P.O. Box 1400, Downers Grove, IL 60515-1426
World Wide Web: www.ivpress.com
E-mail: mail@ivpress.com

InterVarsity Press® is the book-publishing division of InterVarsity Christian Fellowship/USA®, a student movement active on campus at hundreds of universities, colleges and schools of nursing in the United States of America, and a member movement of the International Fellowship of Evangelical Students. For information about local and regional activities, write Public Relations Dept., InterVarsity Christian Fellowship/USA, 6400 Schroeder Rd., P.O. Box 7895, Madison, WI 53707-7895, or visit the IVCF website at <www.intervarsity.org>.

Scripture quotations, unless otherwise noted, are from the New Revised Standard Version of the Bible, copyright 1989 by the Division of Christian Education of the National Council of the Churches of Christ in the USA. Used by permission. All rights reserved.

Design: Cindy Kiple

Images: peonies in garden: Evan Sklar/Getty Images
        hands over paper: Photodisc Collection/Getty Images

ISBN 0-8308-3231-9

Printed in the United States of America ∞

Library of Congress Cataloging-in-Publication Data

Wright, Vinita Hampton, 1958-
  The soul tells a story: engaging creativity with spirituality in
  the writing life / Vinita Hampton Wright.
      p. cm.
  ISBN 0-8308-3231-9 (pbk.: alk. paper)
  1. Creative ability—Religious aspects—Christianity. I. Title.
  BT709.5.W77 2005
  248—dc22

                                                                    2004029589

P	19	18	17	16	15	14	13	12	11	10	9	8	7	6	5	4	3	2	1
Y	19	18	17	16	15	14	13	12	11	10	09	08	07	06	05				

To those who tremble at the power,

wisdom and ecstasy of their gifts:

may you leap into your calling

and feel yourself lifted and healed

in God's mighty arms.

CONTENTS

ACKNOWLEDGMENTS

When I consider all the great books I have read by other artists about writing, art, creativity and the integrated life, this book of mine seems but a term paper—and an early draft at that. Where would I be without Madeleine L'Engle, Annie Dillard, John Gardner, Gregg Levoy, Flannery O'Connor, Ray Bradbury, Natalie Goldberg and the many others who have walked this path ahead of me? Their words have built my courage and deepened my understanding.

Thanks to friends and colleagues who have accompanied me patiently through the mild dramas of creative process as I've written books, put together workshops and struggled with outlines and proposals. Thanks to good writing friends, most of whom are members of the Aphrodite Ladies (you know who you are). And to my agent, Kathryn Helmers, who kept working with me to make this book succeed and to find it a home.

Thanks to all the workshop participants who have given enthusiastic and useful feedback, have added to my understanding of the creative life, and have confirmed that the work I do is worthwhile and helpful.

Thanks to the staff at InterVarsity Press, for believing that the project was worthy and for presenting it to the public in such good style. What a great team to have behind me.

Thanks to my husband, Jim, for enduring daily life with a writing spouse. And to our back-porch neighbors, who—bowl of salad or bottle of wine in hand—help me celebrate every little success.

And thanks to Helen Lundquist, my English teacher, grades six through eight, who helped me embark upon this journey.

A WORD ABOUT BEGINNINGS

I don't even remember now what compelled me to hold my first creativity/spirituality workshop more than three years ago. I think I was just trying to explore it all for myself, and I wanted input from other people. My friend Lil Copan made arrangements for me to try out some material with a group of folks she knew. In the course of discussion, I said something about how we should be able to form ourselves creatively—with intention, that is—and Lil coined the term "creative formation." And that started something. After the discussion was over and she and I were relaxing at day's end, the creative formation topic kept pulling us forward. At some point we decided I should try to write a book.

That is all very foggy, and the story of this book wrote itself, as all stories ultimately do. What you hold in your hands is at least the third version. It was turned down by numerous publishers in its earlier forms. Even after InterVarsity Press decided to do it, there were missing pieces, which IVP's editors and readers identified, and so I did more work. A few years from now I will likely read this and identify yet more pieces that none of us found. With this project I have had to heed my own advice to decide when a thing is finished, even though it's not the masterpiece I once envisioned. I tell myself periodically that it's best if I never meet my expectations; otherwise I would not stretch and learn and wonder appropriately at gifts and inspiration.

I have stayed determined to create this book mainly because workshop participants have shown me again and again that the material is helpful and pertinent. Although I don't pretend that any of this is truly original, I know that much of it is quite important, and if I can help a few creative persons claim their gifts and live more bountifully with them, then I'm satisfied.

I have become a more spiritual person because I write. The creative process is a spiritual one, and when we receive it as such, it deepens our gifts and edifies us in general. To write true stories, I must encounter truth, and as Jesus said, the truth makes us free. It also brings healing and grace when we attend to it. If I truly open my eyes and express in words what I have seen, then I will have participated in a spiritual act. I receive the vision from beyond myself, and I express it through who I am. This is God at work. It may be divinity at its finest, because the whole point of the incarnation was that we understand finally and with clarity who we really are—made in God's image and possessing gifts with which to express God's very self to the world.

And so even with all the heartache of the creative life—the ups and downs, the struggle to understand, the hard work at craft, the impingement of commerce—it can be the most sublime sort of existence. Many days my life is not so sublime, but I encounter joy more now than I ever have, and I give much of the credit to this writing life that has pursued me and that I have chosen to accept as a calling.

I offer this book in thanksgiving as much as anything else. I'm thankful for what I have learned, for what I've been privileged to share with others and for the potential growth of the person who interacts with these pages.

Fiction is the art form of human yearning.

ROBERT OLEN BUTLER, IN *OF FICTION AND FAITH*

People without hope do not write novels. Writing a novel is a terrible experience, during which the hair often falls out and the teeth decay. I'm always highly irritated by people who imply that writing fiction is an escape from reality. It is a plunge into reality and it's very shocking to the system. If the novelist is not sustained by a hope of money, then he must be sustained by a hope of salvation, or he simply won't survive the ordeal.

FLANNERY O'CONNOR, *MYSTERY AND MANNERS*

I am no closer to feeling secure in the world for having lots of answers. Making peace with the questions seems the better bet.

GREGG LEVOY, *CALLINGS*

Writing every book, the writer must solve two problems: Can it be done? and, Can I do it? Every book has an intrinsic impossibility, which its writer discovers as soon as his first excitement dwindles.

ANNIE DILLARD, *THE WRITING LIFE*

At any given moment, the world offers vastly more support to work it already understands—namely, art that's already been around for a generation or a century. Expressions of truly new ideas often fail to qualify as even bad art—they're simply viewed as no art at all.

DAVID BAYLES AND TED ORLAND, *ART AND FEAR*

1 THE HEART-STOPPING ACT OF SAYING YES

What to Expect When You Embrace Creative Callings

I wrote my first "book" during the summer after fourth grade. The title page began on the first sheet of paper in a bright pink spiral-bound notebook, and "The End" appeared on the last sheet; evidently I had already learned something about self-editing for the purpose of page count. I have since been unable to make my literary works come out so precisely.

The title of that first book was "The Gift of the Long Journey," and it was essentially a composite of every *Wagon Train* episode I'd ever watched. It was told in first person by a girl (about my age) who had traveled across the country by wagon train with her parents and her handsome, protective older brother (in real life the author was first-born and had no older brother but wished she did). In the course of the story the heroine got lost, Indians attacked the wagon train, the handsome older brother was wounded but not fatally, and Indians kidnapped the heroine, who escaped by her own wits and bravery. This book is still floating around the family somewhere, which is good. No matter how successful my writing career may become, some sister or nephew will be able to wave around the pink notebook and bring me back to my artistic roots.

My first real book was published when I was forty. Between the fourth grade and age forty I traveled through various jobs and two careers, but all the time I was learning to say yes to that something inside that got abnormally excited about pens and blank notebooks. I always loved office supply stores—that should have been an indication of what inevitably would come. And I read books constantly, almost as much as I watched television. My childhood was a sickly one, and this prevented the sorts of physical activity that many childhoods are made of. It's not surprising that I turned to reading, writing and other pastimes that were physically passive.

But one year, probably during junior high, I read *To Kill a Mockingbird,* and I remember thinking, *I want to write like this. I want to do to people what this writer has just done to me.* That was the real beginning. That day I said yes to my gift. And I have continued to learn, over the years and season by season, what that yes means and how I live it out.

One of the most important powers we have as human beings is the ability to say yes or no. Many of life's pivotal events happen because someone answers a summons, accepts an opportunity or follows a hunch. As a writer I know that saying yes to the next story can feel like any one of these. I also know that in order to say yes to one thing I must nearly always say no to something else. Whatever the case, adrenaline makes its rush through the body, and an otherwise ordinary day takes on the glow of transcendence.

I do believe that creativity involves transcendence. Many a philosopher and theologian has stated that we most resemble the divine when we create. Imagine, then, the power we tap into when we say yes to our creative gifts.

Imagine what *you* tap into when you say yes to your gifts.

You do have creative gifts. They are foundational to your personality, your ability to function from day to day and your life callings. Their discovery may have been delayed by hard times or an oppressive childhood. You may have been denied the opportunity to develop your gifts. But creative gifts are resilient and quite patient. They appear when the time is right and can adapt to an ever-changing environment. Even after being undiscovered or neglected for decades, they can walk onstage in brilliant clothes and dazzle you and those who are your witnesses.

∼ WHAT DOES IT MEAN TO BE CREATIVE?

In a general sense, every human being is creative. This trait is not always flashy. Often it's not called by its true name. But when you take the stuff of life and rearrange it so that it matters, so that it does good things, you're acting creatively. At those times when you are breaking a sweat to make life work better, you are most like the God who created you. You don't have to come up with a new idea in order to be creative. All you have to do is find an old idea and apply it to a new moment or group of people, a new problem or situation.

And so creativity is at work in the parent of preschoolers who must come up with ways of occupying their exuberance for hours, even days, on end. It is also at work in the entrepreneur who can make a buck before she even has a buck. Likewise, the person at the office or the church who never misses an opportunity to make a program or system more effective is exercising creativity. And it's alive and well in the guy who, like my late father, works at a factory job all day and then comes home to tend a garden.

According to the Jewish and Christian story, when God created the world, God made something out of nothing. God spoke the universe into existence. We humans really can't do that. Even when we create new human beings, we start with DNA. But it requires our God-given creative abilities to discover all that has been placed in the universe. Our very act of discovery is true creativity. So often a sculptor will say, as Michelangelo was reported to have done, "I don't make a statue; I chip away the stone until the form inside emerges." The writer will say, "I don't make up characters; I discover them and then listen to their stories." The scientist says, "It's been under our noses for decades, and I know that if I noodle around long enough I'll see it clearly." The parent recognizes suddenly, on a long afternoon, some new wonder in the four-year-old. The sales rep, on the road for the tenth day in a row, sees a connection between product and people that had not occurred until now. Our human life is full of information waiting to be understood and beauty waiting to be unveiled. When we understand and when we unveil, we are living out our creativity.

I make the point that creativity is inherent to human personality because we tend to recognize it only in certain contexts, such as the arts. And when we see it as special to only some people or personality types, it becomes to us a mystery that is often more intimidating than it has to be. The creative process does have its mysterious aspects, but overall it is natural, and we are designed to work with it joyfully and fruitfully. At a basic level, we use our creativity to live within budget or plan a garden plot. At a more specialized level we develop our gifts for mixing colors on a canvas or crafting sentences on a page.

I can't talk with expertise about most forms of creativity. I'm not a parent, I'm really bad with numbers and technical things, I am science deficient, and I don't have a green thumb. Neither can I paint, dance, act or build. I dabble in music. Mostly I write stories.

So I am going to form this book mainly within the context of the writing art. But I will also be drawing on what I have heard and read from people who are in what we call the fine arts—other writers, painters, sculptors, photographers, dancers and musicians. Most of these people live the creative life quite intentionally. They have tuned in more carefully than most of us to the specific characteristics and stages of creativity. So I will use primarily their terms in exploring the creative process.

I will also use my own experience and background. My faith tradition is Christian, and I will make several references to how my tradition has affected and continues to affect my creative life. I'm sure there will be certain parallels between my experience and yours, regardless of your tradition.

There are two main purposes to this book. One is to help you identify your own creative process and learn how to participate with it more fully. There is mystery, and there is practicality. There is revelation, and there is simple practice. I hope to make all of this a little easier to think about and work with.

The second purpose is to help make the connection between your spiritual life and your creative work. After years of writing, and particularly since I have written fiction on a regular basis, I've become convinced that creative work is spiritual at its heart. And I believe that much can be gained if we attend to spirituality along with creativity. I have asked people to consider carefully how these two aspects of life relate for them, and it's been encouraging, and sometimes surprising, how eagerly people have discussed both of these topics in the same conversation. Many of us sense that our soul has become fragmented by the cultural (and personal) separation of creativity from spirituality, and we want to experience them in greater integration.

WHAT IS THE CREATIVE LIFE?

When we say yes to our gifts, it's good for us to know at least some of what we're saying yes to. Each creative life writes its unique story. But some aspects of creativity seem to be common and consistent.

Creativity Is Exploratory

This gets more artists into more trouble than any other aspect of creative work. Artists are put on earth to explore, to push the boundaries, to ask yet more questions, and sometimes to do away with—or at least challenge—traditional assumptions.

This trait can look like rebellion or simple contrariness, but it is in fact the nature of creativity. Creativity looks for a new way to say or depict something that's been around forever. Every day we must rise and go about our life, and if creativity did not provide fresh ways in which to perceive our experiences and articulate them, we would grow dull and tired and aimless very quickly.

Each generation must learn the same truths as every generation that came before. And in order for that to happen, new incarnations must occur in every aspect of life—music, art, literature, education, religion, medicine, politics and so on. We must constantly think of new ways to embrace the world.

This exploring of the boundaries is why we can discover how to transplant hearts; it is why the theory of relativity is articulated. Exploration is how we can progress from black and white to Technicolor and the reason we finally came up with a name for postpartum depression. Life demands that we be willing to let go of one belief so that a larger, truer belief can take its place. This is frightening business, and sometimes it makes us uncomfortable or even angry.

And so, with great regularity, some artist's vision attracts a crowd of protesters, or a movie is boycotted, or a book is banned. Galileo gets dragged to the Inquisitor; Mozart dies a pauper. All of these scenarios occur because people creatively explore the world and in so doing disturb others. They convey the old truths in new forms and languages. They are driven to do this. Creative work actually brings on society's growing pains. It is anything but risk free.

When you embark upon creative work, it will push your personal boundaries. It will open up parts of yourself with which you have been unfamiliar. It will cause you to ask questions of your life. It will insist that you come up with names for things that until now you haven't examined carefully at all.

The exploratory nature of creativity makes it scary at times. But it also adds intrigue and sizzle to life and moves the mundane into a realm of wonder.

Creativity Is Whole-Life Engagement

You can't engage with a creative process and not engage other processes. When you are exploring and unveiling, your emotions get hooked, your intellect gets hooked, and your deepest beliefs about life get hooked. If creativity is nurtured well and allowed to grow, it will grab onto your life in multiple ways.

Much of the creative flatness that surrounds us exists precisely because people have been willing to nurture one part of life but not another. They may write songs that are lovely but not very original: rather than explore and find new incarnations—which involves a spiritual, philosophical risk—they stick with the proven formulas of former eras. The financial bottom line may keep artists employing fine craft but choosing forms that have ceased to be emotionally alive; they are too pat to elicit much response. Sometimes artists avoid certain subject matters out of simple fear. For instance, writers who hail from a restrictive religious subculture may neuter their stories, excising any sexual content or energy in order to conform to boundaries set by religious peers.

The most powerful art speaks to its audience on many different levels. It engages the physical senses by providing specific, concrete information. It engages the emotions by being relevant to people's desires. It engages our thoughtful, philosophical nature by having some form and underlying hypothesis. It engages our spiritual sensibilities because it has been formed in a person's spiritual core, thereby touching on life's transcendent character. It engages our sexuality because it respects our need for connection—even if the creative piece itself explores alienation.

As you get in touch with your creative gifts, you will, as a matter of course, get in touch with every facet of your being. A particular poem will call up memories of your past, or a painting will bloom once you engage a fuller range of emotions. A character in your novel or play will finally open up when you delve into that character's sexual identity or spiritual beliefs—and in delving into those things you will touch your own sexuality and spirituality.

So prepare yourself for full-life engagement. You can embrace this work and never be bored again. Or you can resist it and suffer one of two fates: you yourself will become numb and boring, or you will exist in that nerve-jangling tension of never quite saying yes or no.

Creativity Can Be Participated in but Not Controlled

In creative work you are uncovering reality that transcends your sensibilities. Whatever you reveal about life through your own work will by its very nature touch on the revelations of other works by other people. And so you are joining in a process that unfolds in your life but it is not confined to your experience. The most you can do is participate; you will never run the show.

Mature artists have learned that they cannot control the process by which they create. They can embrace it; they can acquiesce to it; they can marvel at it; they can enjoy the ride. Their only control lies in the mastery of their craft. For instance, it is up to me to master the intricacies of structure, style, grammar and all that goes into the writing art. But I can't sit down and simply decide how a story is going to unfold. I don't yet know how the story will unfold. I very likely don't even know how the story will end. That's because *unfold* is the operative word. I can pay attention and witness the unfolding, and then, if I have mastered my craft, I can capture what unfolds and communicate it to others.

Our creative work issues from our memories and our subconscious, from stories that predate us, from matters that are so deep and so important that we cannot contain them at any one time. This work requires a process that is larger and wiser than we are. We should be very grateful that we can't control it, because we wouldn't be up to the job anyway.

Creativity May Involve an Artistic Temperament—and It May Not

When we see the terms *artist* and *creative*, we tend to think of the most flamboyant representatives of these two categories. A personality such as Pyotr Ilich Tchaikovsky or Pablo Picasso is quite publicity friendly—and also translates well into movie rights. We think of Ernest Hemingway or Andy Warhol or Martha Graham when someone says "artist."

But some of the most creative people do not look artistic at all. They work long hours and are quite practical and unromantic. Have you talked lately with someone who organizes relief efforts after an earthquake has ripped apart an entire region? You don't get any more creative than that, and yet such people appear to be more pragmatic than creative.

Forget about the stereotypes. Some creative people can be recognized as such from a mile away. Others practice their creative gifts day in and day out but no one would ever think to call them artists.

Maybe you have an artistic temperament, and maybe you don't. That really doesn't matter. What is important is that you discover your creative gifts and develop them.

✎ Do You Need to Identify or Redefine Your Gifts?

Many people grow up with a good understanding of the tasks they do well. If a child is lucky, her innate gifts are nurtured from an early age. Daddy makes sure there's always plenty of paper and colored markers for her to play with. Mom takes her outside often and just lets her explore the world. Grandma funds music lessons when the little boy begins to mimic tunes in perfect pitch. Some of us are very fortunate in this way. My family had no money to speak of during my childhood. But Dad subscribed to a children's book club for years so that each month we received a new book. When I began to sound out tunes on the piano at age six, my parents convinced the junior high music teacher to stop by once a week and give me lessons. If my sisters or I ever wrote a story or had a song to perform, there was an audience and much encouragement.

Not everyone has this kind of nurture. And even where creative activities are encouraged as a pastime, the vision of a creative vocation may have been missing. Though I was encouraged in my creative endeavors, no one in my family nudged me toward a writing career, because none of them knew anyone who made a living at writing. It was assumed that I would become a music teacher. I went through college as a music major, writing on the side and taking every elective writing class I could squeeze in. After nearly a decade of training to be a music teacher and holding teaching jobs, it finally occurred to me that my truest, deepest love was writing.

You may not have been nurtured toward creativity. Or you may have been nurtured in one direction but not another. You may have been pushed by peer pressure or family pressure or simple financial pressure toward a career that lay far from your creative gifts. And you may stay in that career for a lot of good reasons.

In some families, the most important thing is to have a career that will support you well financially. This is nothing to sniff at. I'm a writer now, but I paid my dues through a decade of full-time editorial work. People tend to be more creative when they are eating reasonably well and not hiding from creditors. We have to prioritize needs and tasks and make choices accordingly.

But creative gifts exist apart from jobs and careers. A lot of people have "day jobs" and still carry on with their creative work. Whether or not you make a living by using your creative gifts is beside the point. Right now, this day, you can ask yourself, *Am I really developing my creative gifts? Have I identified them fully?*

Even if you've identified a general gift such as writing, perhaps it's time to go further. You're comfortable writing for newspapers, but now you're itching to try poetry or fiction. Your friend has been asking you to do some script writing; that's not your field and so you've always declined the request, but perhaps you want to say yes. There is always more to know about your own gifts, more to identify and develop.

Look Back for the Clues

We naturally concentrate on one or two of our gifts, most likely because they come more easily or the opportunity is there. But there is likely other giftedness yet to be discovered. If you're at all foggy about what your gifts are or which gifts are begging for attention, you can start where you are, with your present interests. What do you enjoy doing? If you have a spare hour or two, what are you inclined to do with it?

Think back a decade or two. What did you enjoy when you were in college or high school or elementary school? When you had time and not so many commitments, what did you enjoy? What classes really turned you on—woodworking? choir? foreign languages? It's possible that important clues have gotten buried in layers of jobs, relationships, business commitments and schedules.

Think back even further to what you loved as a child. What gave you joy before anyone told you what you should be doing or liking? Just a few years ago I realized that I have been writing stories and making books since early childhood. I made scrapbooks out of pictures I cut out of magazines, and then I wrote words that went with the pictures. See, I was an editor and writer way back when. What were *you* way back when?

Follow Your Joy
What really gives you joy? Creative work that is fruitful is long term, exhausting and many leveled. There are easier ways to get a paycheck. So I find that people who have settled into creative work have stuck with it for one reason: it gives them joy. At the very least they experience a level of satisfaction that keeps them engaged over time.

This joy occurs during the process as well as in response to the finished work. For every finished novel a writer produces, a half-dozen others remain unfinished—or finished—in a file cabinet. Most of them won't get published because there's some flaw or because the subject matter won't sell. But the writer works on them anyway, because to do so satisfies something at the soul level.

So consider what gives you joy, deep down. Mythologist and author Joseph Campbell would ask, "What is your bliss?" Creativity researcher Mihaly Csikszentmihalyi would ask, "Where is the flow?" We do best what we do joyfully. And when we find what we truly love, we can develop the gifts that allow us to indulge in this love more consistently.

Even the Christian Scriptures recognize the element of joy in giftedness. The Greek word *charism* has to do with joy, and this word is used throughout St. Paul's discussion of spiritual gifts (1 Corinthians 12).

Talk to Your Friends

The people who spend a lot of time with you, who have lived with you and dealt with you for years, know you better than you'd like to think. Ask a chosen four or five people what they think your gifts are. They probably won't have to stand there and think; most likely they'll respond quickly and offer examples to back up what they say.

Your gifts are sometimes more obvious to others than they are to you. And you are likely more critical of yourself than other people are of you. One of the biggest obstacles to embracing your gifts is that inner critic who has already decided that you have no talent. Your loved ones are not saddled with your inner critic. They are free to simply look at your life and report what they see.

Listen to what people say, and then take the information for what it's worth. If you ask your mother, she may give it to you straight—or she may slant her response to suit her own dreams for you. Any person will have biases, and he will couch his response in terms that fit his concept of gifts and creativity. But there will be some evidence in what he observes about your abilities.

Take Note of Others' Responses

Pay attention to how other people respond to your creative work. A true gift gives true pleasure to others—or it truly stirs them up. When your friend's face lights up while he's talking about some endeavor of yours, you know that somehow that endeavor really connected to another person. When people have a strong reaction to your work, positive or negative, that tells you that you've hit on something that's meaningful.

Cooking is one of my creative gifts, and I try to throw a couple of big dinner parties every year. After one of them a friend said, "I've never seen you so relaxed and happy as when you were in the kitchen, right in the middle of everything." I'd never thought of myself as relaxed—putting on a multicourse dinner for fourteen people certainly has its stresses. But this friend saw evidence that I was doing what I am gifted to do.

When people are moved and helped by what you do, that means something. Don't take compliments lightly; store them up. Review them. Really listen to what it is people are getting out of what you do. This information is important to you.

For years I regretted my tendency to be an outsider. I never felt comfortable in crowds or at parties, and I didn't naturally build large networks of friends. An introvert always has to work harder to connect with others than more outgoing folks do. And as a writer, I was nearly always the observer, the person who attended the party but simply watched everyone else there.

Then I published two novels, and I began to hear from people. And I realized that people perceived my love through my storytelling. People connected with the stories and felt loved or understood or encouraged through them. So maybe I'm more of an observer than a party animal, but that doesn't mean that I am uninvolved with people. I've stopped feeling guilty about my introversion, because I know that it's part of my writing gift, necessary to it in fact. And the writing gift that I indulged on the sly for years has become one of my best means for loving others.

What do you offer to people that makes them feel loved or encouraged or hopeful? What do people look forward to receiving from you? What are the best gifts you bring to a gathering of friends? In the Christian tradition, gifts are considered to be equipment God has given us in order to build up and help others. Pay attention to how others pay attention to you. This will help you zero in on your gifts.

✎ WHAT HAPPENS WHEN YOU SAY YES TO CREATIVE GIFTS?

I was a fearful child who grew up to be a fearful adult. I said my biggest yes to creativity only after I'd gone through several life upheavals and learned that I could survive risk and change. At a certain point I just decided that being safe was not God's only ambition for me, and it was no longer my primary ambition. A lot of life was waiting to unfold, and I realized it would do so only when I engaged with my own soul more honestly and courageously.

I decided that I would write no matter what. That involved a career change, but that was merely the outward shift. A lot of other things happened too. I'm so glad they did, but I sympathize with people who hesitate before saying yes. It's always a bigger step than it appears.

What have you let yourself in for when you say yes to the creative part of your life?

Much of what follows won't be new information. You will likely recognize situations that you have already experienced. Remember that you're not alone.

Expect to Be Misunderstood

People who are not yet acquainted with their creativity will think you're odd. If you're fully invested in a creative vision, then they'll suspect that you're imbalanced. If they really admire what you're doing, they may go the other extreme and hold you in awe. Either way, you are misunderstood. Whether your calling is to write novels or to help form cooperatives in Third World countries, you will encounter prejudice.

Perfectly fine people will think you are wasting your life if you don't get a real job that gives you a nice retirement package. Perfectly loving friends and family members will keep waiting for you to grow up and get over this phase. Well-intentioned religious folks will worry about your dealing with dark and uncomfortable topics. You're not going to escape these reactions. It's up to you to find loving responses to them. Concentrate on people's intentions rather than their aggravating theories and comments.

When people hear that I'm writing a story, they usually assume there's some agenda. They wonder what "the point" is. They react with confusion when I say that I'm merely exploring a certain theme through these characters—that there is "no point," at least not at the beginning. In our culture good, conscientious people come up with plans, steps and objectives. They are not conditioned to think in terms of a transcendent process. So any answers I give that don't line up with an action plan create awkward silences in the conversation. I don't take offense at this, but I assume that the only people who will really understand my creative life are those who are engaged in their own.

Expect to Scare Some People

Your willingness to grapple with questions will unnerve people who banned serious questions from their life years ago. Your tendency to bump into dark, shadowy things will convince some people that you're losing your religious bearings; their religious practice has been to avoid dealing with any darkness at all, beyond labeling as evil anything that makes them uncomfortable.

Staid religious people, staunchly rational people and unawakened people may feel nervous the moment you enter the room. All you can do is be gentle. Speak their language as best you can. Share your life with care. For instance, if you have been energized by talking with a practitioner of some other religious tradition, it will be best not to enthuse about it during coffee hour at First Fundamentalist Church. We've all known people who seemed to enjoy stirring up trouble and making people uncomfortable on purpose. That's just childish.

Sooner or later, though, you will question the status quo. Artists and Old Testament prophets are alike in this; they often see what others can't or won't see, and once they see, they can't keep quiet about it. And people who need the security of the status quo will simply come unhinged in response. There's nothing you can do about it.

The explorations that occur naturally in your life will always be frightening to people who are not in the same place. Don't get angry at their fearfulness. Listen to what they are saying, because they are part of your community and have a right to voice their concerns. Don't be surprised to encounter some fervent reactions to your temperament, process and creations.

Expect to Be Rejected

My gifts were always welcomed and encouraged in my family, church and school communities. What was not welcomed was the personality from which those gifts sprang. I was moody, easily depressed and extremely introverted. I had no social skills, was too honest when I talked, and didn't know anything about flirtation or other forms of politics. Instead I dove into the shadow sides of traits that made me artistic. I wasn't trying to do that, but it's what happened naturally. I was a stormy, unhappy person during much of my formation. This was due partly to the temperament that made me gifted. But it was due also to my overriding sense that people didn't accept me as I was.

And no one seemed to understand how to help me grow into the more positive traits. I didn't learn to balance the storminess until I was well into my twenties. It's a shame no one was able to help me earlier.

Most people responded to me as though I chose to be closed off and depressed. I would be told to stop having a long face, that I should smile more, that I should be more outgoing, that if I'd stop dwelling on negative things I wouldn't be depressed all the time. Because I was painfully shy, peers assumed that I was stuck up. People tried to "help" me by attacking the manifestations rather than getting to the reasons for them. The result was that I didn't feel loved but quite rejected. And that hurt enough to make me resistant to any of the "solutions" that were offered.

It didn't help when my religious mentors—pastors and teachers—approached my negative traits more as sins to be overcome than as shadow sides of a gifted personality. To be outgoing and other-oriented was the correct spiritual gift. To be inward was to be self-centered. To their credit, the people who were leaders to me during college had at least educated themselves a bit about varieties of temperaments, and that was helpful. But the knowledge was far from being integrated.

My creativity was always closely connected to my spirituality, and this made things somewhat easier than they would have been otherwise. During my teens and twenties, my creativity manifested through songs, stories and plays that were directly connected to my faith journey. This not only alleviated some of the rejection but earned some praise from religious peers. From early childhood I was hooked into an awareness of spiritual life. And so the spiritual interests overrode the creative ones. However, when creativity became a stronger force in my life, some rejection came with it.

The creative process often leads to temporary imbalances that other people may not tolerate well. There's some craziness to the creative life. You may be terrifically energetic for a time and then shift to low energy and mild depression. Some of this flux goes with the territory. There are times when you need help with the imbalance because it has become unhealthy or dangerous. But today's culture values a certain perception of "balance," and it allows for little craziness or fluctuation. People will reject your apparent imbalances as negatives that need to be corrected. And when you don't share their concern, they will likely judge you, which is a form of rejection.

Creativity takes you places that are weird to others. Don't be surprised when others reject you for being different, asking too many questions or expressing yourself in ways that are unfamiliar to them.

Expect to Lose Control
Creativity is like an impish spirit. It is a magician, a prophet, a shape changer. You'll think you've got the plot figured out. Then all of a sudden your writing brings you to a door that you're fool enough to open, and there's a whole room of unforeseen stuff that you must deal with

now. Get used to this. The wonder of creative life is that it is connected
to a spiritual life in which forces besides you are operating.

Your subconscious mind is up all night figuring out what it is that
your conscious mind is avoiding, and when your creative self hooks
into the subconscious, here come surprises. This is the way it is supposed to work. This is also why true creativity is so powerful: it brings
us to places our rational selves wouldn't go to willingly, and it does so
in a way that we can handle. If somebody calls me a hypocrite, I'll get
mad and stomp away. But if my hypocritical self confronts me through
a character in a short story, I will read and be moved and want to be a
better person. It's powerful and crafty and wonderful. But it's never
predictable, for the person who creates or for the people who witness
what has been created.

Not only do you lose control by entering the creative process, you
lose control once others have witnessed your work. Their perceptions
of it—and reactions to it—will happen completely outside your
realm. What your work accomplishes in other people is outside your
control as well. I often refer to my novels as children who have grown
up and left home. Who knows what they're really doing out in the
world? I receive reports from time to time, and I'm happy when
they're good reports. But all I can do is wait for some word of activity.

Just accept that much of the time you're swimming in water way
over your head, that you are out of your realm, that this whole thing
is happening in a language you don't recognize. Think of it as fun.

There are also a lot of good things waiting for you when you say yes
to your gifts. Here are just a few.

Expect to Grow More Intuitive

Your creativity will bring you into closer and more frequent contact
with those parts of your soul that don't get a lot of attention in daily
life. You may become more aware of dreams and memories. You will
likely learn to recognize your hunches and become more willing to
follow them. You will probably become better at reading other people.

These things happen when we exercise the intuition that makes creativity possible.

Some people become a little more mystical when they engage in creativity. Creative work will demonstrate to you again and again that the world is bigger and deeper than you perceive, that God has many ways of speaking to your soul, and that the soul itself possesses much wisdom that you simply hadn't noticed before.

Expect to Become More Attentive to, and Engaged with, Life

Creative work teaches you to pay attention, and this is something that few people do well or often. We spend hours and days at a time just trying to get ahead of an impossible schedule or solve one of many problems. We don't have time to sit and watch what light does to the color of the living-room wall at a certain time in the afternoon. Well, if you are painting a picture with a living-room wall in it, you'll learn to notice your wall. Or if you're writing a story that contains an afternoon scene, you will pay better attention to what physical qualities make the afternoon different from morning or evening.

Engagement goes hand in hand with attentiveness. Once you truly attend to the details of life, you will learn how to deal with them intentionally and thoughtfully. Artists talk of being in the flow or losing track of time. This happens when our senses, mind and emotions are completely occupied with the task at hand. Creative work, particularly work done regularly rather than sporadically, leads you right into engagement.

In Christian devotional language, *engagement* involves living in the moment or finding God in the ordinary. You have little choice but to live in the moment when you are doing creative work. And the ordinary regularly opens up to become extraordinary. This is just one way in which creativity enhances the spiritual life; it gives excellent training in attentiveness and living in the moment.

Expect to Acquire Wisdom and Humor

I have attended so many writers' and publishers' conferences over the years that they blend together in my memory. To tell the truth, if you've attended one, you've attended most of them. But I keep going, even when my job as an editor does not require it. Why? As a group, writers are not particularly flamboyant; many of us are rather introverted. However, once I'm in conversation with a few of these people, I remember why I stay in this business. Creative types are simply interesting to be around.

When you work with ideas, dreams, visions, intuition and other soul matters day in and day out, you can't help but grow in wisdom. Your interest in life is constantly aroused. You yourself are interesting because you are so engaged with the world. Even if you're an emotional artistic type, you give your brain cells lots of practice. You're an aware person.

Most artists I know have a well-developed sense of humor. They see the irony and strangeness of life. They recognize connections that others miss. They have learned to take joy in small, ordinary things. When I'm at the dinner table with other writers, we laugh as much as we talk. And I believe that this is a very good quality to have.

So if you are embarking on the creative journey, know that your mind will grow sharper and your heart bigger. Even as you navigate periods of depression and anxiety, you will become more ready to laugh and to receive joy wherever you find it.

Expect to Understand God in Broader and Deeper Ways

All the time I encounter artists who have weathered various changes in their spirituality because of their growth as artists. My own story is not so unusual. As I developed my art, I engaged more deeply with parts of the personality that operate in creativity. I had grown up in a Christian tradition that was void of liturgy or ritual. My tradition had a pretty standoffish relationship with mystery too. But the more writing I did, the more I bumped into mystery and the more I felt it was necessary to a well-rounded faith. The more attentive I became toward life in general, the more important life's physicality became to me, and I began to feel a need for ritual and sacred objects. The more I realized that my art connected me with other people, the more I longed for liturgy, in which worshipers participate together very intentionally.

In the course of ordinary growth, people often gravitate toward aspects of faith and practice with which they are not as familiar. I attended one nondenominational church that was filled with evangelicals hungering for more liturgy and Catholics longing for more Bible study. Creative work moves us toward the bigger picture, the more complete puzzle. It helps us fill in the parts that have been missing.

This is one reason many artists who come from established faith traditions waver when the time comes to walk through a new door to the next creative work. They know that they will be changed by the work itself. The fear comes from the assumption that change is bad. I've been a Christian for more than three decades, and my faith has undergone numerous changes, but I look at that history now and see all the change as growth.

Years ago J. B. Phillips wrote a book titled *Your God Is Too Small*. He explained how humans tend to create God in the images they know best—such as the overly harsh father or the resident policeman or the managing director. Not only do people create their personal images of God, but branches of Christianity create images as well. This is inevitable, because humans need stability and clear definitions. But thanks to artists, theologians, philosophers and various other saints, those definitions are constantly questioned, tweaked and expanded. God will always be bigger and deeper than any religious vision or theological construct.

If you follow the path to your creative gifts, you will encounter again and again your own beliefs, desires, prayers, frailties and epiphanies. Growth is made of all these things. And God watches over us as we walk that path, offering guidance and grace.

WHAT WILL SPIRITUAL AWARENESS REQUIRE FROM YOUR CREATIVE LIFE?

The spiritual life makes its demands too. Your spirituality is taking you on a journey, and that journey is never simple or easy. As your creativity develops, you are hooking into spiritual realities that are new to you yet that were mapped out long before you discovered them.

It is safe to say that all the items I listed in the section on following your creativity can apply to following your spirituality. You will be misunderstood, feared and rejected. Ask any saint. You will also become more intuitive, wise and willing to laugh. And as you treat your creative journey and spiritual journey as one and the same, you can expect further developments.

Expect to Be Harder on Yourself

Your spirit—that place where faith and choice collide—is determined to grow you into the marvelous person God has had in mind all along. This person is someone with grace, love, courage, compassion, faith and integrity. You don't become this without some work and suffering. The spirit will require tougher things than the Muse ever will. The spirit will not be satisfied when you merely embrace your personal darkness and write an astounding poem about it; the spirit will push you beyond that to whatever healing or understanding is necessary in your life.

This spirit will stare at you until you make your art honest. The spirit will sit quietly in the corner until you rewrite that character to be the true character rather than what you might want him or her to be. The spirit will require that you push through the despair and get to the hope, that you push past the comfort and embrace the confession.

Expect to Live Within Certain Parameters

Creative people often balk when any kind of system or limit is placed on them. When you feel that you were born to explore the edges and test the limits, you don't want to be told to live within them. But if you have surrendered yourself to the God of the universe, you are giving God permission to throw up a fence whenever God wants to throw up a fence. There are times when you need the protection of a fence, and you must trust your Creator to know when that is.

You may stumble onto a real demon when you're down in the basement hunting for the right scene or symbol. Your spirit may say, "You're not ready to wrestle with this yet; leave it alone." Or, "Go ahead and write this play. But get some moral support, because the going will get rough."

When you are attentive to the spiritual dynamics of your life, you don't do something just because you can. You don't create a work of art simply to create a sensation. You do it because the time is right. You do it because your own growth requires it. You do it because you have discovered a new way to see something that might help others see it too. You do it because the community of which you are a part needs for you to do it. That doesn't mean that the community is always ready for it; sometimes the Spirit uses art to upset us and make us search ourselves. But the artist who follows the spirit is sensitive to doing the right work at the right time.

Expect to Make Sacrifices for the Sake of Love
Here I must speak from a Christian bias, although this view is certainly not exclusive to Christianity. I believe that love is the supreme requirement in all situations. My creativity is important, but it is not important enough to veto the choices made by love. The person who is integrating her creative gifts with the life of the spirit will defer to love.

We know the stories of great creative people who have sacrificed wives, husbands, children, friends and careers in order to pursue their work. These situations are always complex, and it's not up to us to make judgments about what the artist should or should not have done. But I believe that there are ways to fulfill my creative callings without violating my callings of relationship. And because I am convinced that my creative gifts were given to me by God, I can trust that somehow or other I will be able to do the work I am called to do. I must trust also that if for some reason I am unable to complete one work, another will rise to take its place. Because I am working in what is essentially a spiritual realm, the possibilities for my creative life are far beyond what I will ever exhaust in my lifetime. I can afford to lose an opportunity here and there, as other circumstances require it.

Families break under all sorts of strains and trials; I doubt that strong marriages end simply because people follow their gifts. Relationships are fragile and must be nurtured through creative surges, job changes, family illness or death, and children's crises. And because the world is broken and imperfect, there are times when, for the sake of loving others well, your creativity will have to wait. And yes, that poem may never come to you again; you may lose it entirely. That book may never get written if you don't write it now. Losses are precisely that—you lose something and you won't get it back. If your marriage is in crisis, you may lose that painting because all of your soul's energy is called upon to mend your marriage. If your child or parent becomes ill and must be cared for long term, you may not sit at your computer for months, and some other writer with fewer burdens will write the book you wanted to write.

Good life is costly. If you are guided by awareness of and responsiveness to your spiritual calling, you will make sacrifices, and sometimes those sacrifices will involve the creative gifts you love so much. When that happens, all you can do is leave the situation in the hands of your Creator, who will hold all of it—the giftedness, the glory, the sacrifices, the losses. Ultimately we must trust these things to God's care and let them go.

Expect to Lose Control

Your creativity will take you places you don't intend, and the spiritual life will do the same. Give up the illusion that you're in charge. The best you can do is develop your gifts with all the strength and mind and heart you have. Become a master at your craft. That way, when the path shifts upward suddenly or veers off to another story line, you'll have the practiced ability to manage it and handle the material responsibly.

The spiritual life is invariably sprinkled with sojourns in the wilderness, and such excursions will affect your creative work. Dark nights of the soul, long days in the desert, sudden fogs of depression—these are out of your control. You usually can't do anything to prevent them or make them end sooner. The blessing of nurturing your creative life, though, is that often you can use your gifts to explore the hell you're going through. Such exploration may not relieve the suffering, but it can form wisdom and strength in you.

Do You Choose This Life, or Does It Choose You?

Once you have identified and accepted your creative gifts, you can move forward. You can gather information about the life of the spirit and of creativity. You can enter a process, very intentionally, in order to develop your gifts. If you have come this far, you've already done a great deal. You've done more than a lot of people have. You know that you are on a particular course, one that is yours alone.

At some point you will recognize that not only have you chosen this course of development and giftedness, but this life has chosen you. You are in fact being called to a life of creativity. Your gifts are making requirements of you.

We assume that we have some sort of control over our destiny, that everything lies in the choices we make. And to a great extent that is true. But our choices are always in response to Something Else. We are called to a life, to a work, to a dream, to our gifts. This calling is much bigger than us. We must commit ourselves to potential we don't even know about yet.

Maybe you thought you were getting into a creative activity because it would be a fun hobby. Or you thought you could get an article published in a magazine or you could step onto the stage of the local theater. Maybe you just liked the idea of getting your hands dirty building homes or tending a garden. In the beginning it may have felt like a whim or a diversion. Oops!—you have now encountered that great core of promise, your inner house of rooms full of divine gifts. And now the hobby is saying to you, "So are you truly interested in what you can do? That vision that's keeping you awake nights—are you ready to see it appear in real life? Well, pace yourself. It's commitment time."

Once it's commitment time, you might find yourself approaching something huge, such as a career change. Then again, your commitment may entail something as simple as allowing yourself one more hour every week to do what you really enjoy doing. Whatever the commitment is, it is right for you. More important, it is possible.

Much more becomes possible when you realize the spiritual components of your creative gifts. You are not merely developing abilities that lie within the range of your experience and training; you are tapping something that is deeper and broader. Furthermore, your creativity relies on more than you; you get to share the responsibility.

Saying yes to your gifts is a huge thing to do. It's no wonder that some people never quite get to yes. It helps to remember that you are saying yes to the work itself and not to any particular outcome. You are not saying yes to a successful career as a novelist; you are merely saying yes to writing—and you may not write novels but end up in another genre entirely. The important thing is that you have made a commitment to your gifts and are willing to see where that commitment takes you.

❧ EXERCISES FOR A WRITER'S FORMATION

Name Your Gifts

For the next five minutes, write about what gave you joy as a child. Write quickly without analyzing or editing.

Take another five minutes and describe the most glorious or satisfying event of your high school life.

Try to remember the last time you were involved with a project that so captivated your attention that you lost track of time. What were you doing?

If five people closest to you—whether friends or family—were to tell you honestly what good things you have brought to their lives, what qualities or gifts would they list?

Complete These Sentences

The activity that gives me greatest joy is . . .
The good qualities that best describe my life are . . .
The help that people often solicit from me is . . .
The part of my personality that I would most hate to lose is . . .
The work that is most satisfying to me is . . .
The activity that I feel drawn to, even when it's scary, is . . .

Consider the Cost

Write a paragraph about what saying yes to your gift has already meant for you.

Write a paragraph about what you fear saying yes might cost you.

Name, as specifically as you can, the gift that seems to be calling to you most consistently or urgently right now.

In one sentence, articulate what you plan to do that will say yes in a new or more intense way.

The artist goes back to the chaos and the ways in which it is experienced, moment to moment through our sense, and pulls out bits and pieces of that sensual experience. The artist gives it back to the reader reshaped. In selecting and shaping and structuring the sensual experience, the artist creates a vision of order for the reader, not as an idea, not as a set of principles, but as a kind of harmonic that's set up in the reader, a resonance.

ROBERT OLEN BUTLER, IN *OF FICTION AND FAITH*

Everything is gestation and then bringing forth. To let each impression and each germ of a feeling come to completion wholly in itself, in the dark, in the inexpressible, the unconscious, beyond the reach of one's own intelligence, and await with deep humility and patience the birth-hour of a new clarity: that alone is living the artist's life: in understanding as in creating.

RAINER MARIA RILKE, *LETTERS TO A YOUNG POET*

It is . . . on the level of the imagination that we formulate our initial response to the encounter with the divine; faith finds expression first as myth and ritual, sacrament, symbol, image and story. Only later does it become dogma and institution.

KATHLEEN R. FISCHER, *THE INNER RAINBOW*

Our religious vision must be translated into the unique voice of a particular epoch if it is to support a living faith. For this translation we depend on the artists of our age.

KATHLEEN R. FISCHER, *THE INNER RAINBOW*

Art and spirituality are nevertheless similar in that both are sets of activities that infuse all aspects of a person's life and gradually shape that person's worldview.

ROBERT WUTHNOW, *CREATIVE SPIRITUALITY*

2 THE JOURNEY OF CREATIVE FORMATION

How to Approach Your Gifts with Faith and Intention

At age eleven or so, I wrote my first song. I was sitting at my bedroom window with a tiny half-keyboard electric organ in front of me. Outside the window, in the summer afternoon, my younger sister was playing with two neighbor kids. While fooling around, I hit upon a nice progression, and it sounded so pretty that I thought I should put words to it. Maybe because the neighbor kids, just yards away, came from a pretty bleak home and my upbringing had taught me to see such people as needing Jesus, I came up with lyrics that were about Jesus as a friend and Savior. In a short time I had a full melody and two or three verses. I sang it for my parents, who, being the good parents they were, responded with praise and a little bit of awe.

Once that happened, I just kept going. I wrote Jesus songs all through junior high and high school. Adolescence is intense in many ways, and for me it was a time of fervent spirituality. I spent hours at the piano composing, pouring my heart into songs that served as prayers, because I felt too odd, unworthy or self-conscious to just sit and talk to the air. Music made the process more natural. This was also how I articulated my theology; a lot of these songs were based on verses or passages from the Bible.

The 1970s was the era of the Jesus Movement, an evangelical Christian response to the countercultural movement of the 1960s. Whereas the hippies practiced free love, sex, drugs and rock 'n' roll, the Jesus freaks practiced agape love, abstained from sex and drugs, and co-opted rock 'n' roll by giving it different lyrics. I was young enough to be just behind the Jesus Movement wave, but even in rural Kansas I was surrounded by the new Christian music: Phil Keaggy, Love Song, Second Chapter of Acts and Larry Norman. And there was Nancy Honeytree, a slender girl with long hair who wore glasses, played guitar and sang songs about Jesus—a woman I could relate to.

It was also the era of the charismatic movement, and I was involved with a number of charismatic Christians during high school. So I performed my songs at camp meetings and in churches where the "elders" were in their thirties and looked essentially like 1960s children only without the glassy eyes or the anger. A couple of these elders believed that I might be the next Honeytree and made sure I was included in events where my emerging talents could be showcased.

During college I wrote good lyrics and passable music while putting on little concerts for churches and community organizations. I had found the perfect marriage between my artistic gifts and blossoming faith. By the time I finished this composer-lyricist phase in my late twenties, I'd written 120 songs or so. A handful of them had commercial possibilities, but I wasn't up to the sort of self-promotion that this would have required. And although I had a good voice, it was never good enough for performance and in fact began failing on me later when I was teaching public school.

However good or mediocre those songs and performances may have been, they always elicited genuine response from the audiences. In a Baptist church, a genuine response is a hearty, corporate "Amen!" at the conclusion of a performance, often with applause. But it usually went further than that, with individuals coming up to me afterward and thanking me for what I'd written. Sometimes they would be tearful, and sometimes they would tell me some of their own story.

Along the way I realized that my songs somehow opened people to confide in me as they probably should have confided in a pastor. All I could do was be gracious. I've had to conclude that since my musical abilities were limited, something beyond musicianship must have been happening. I didn't set out to write songs that I thought people would like. I merely transformed my prayers into songs, and as it turned out, my prayers were a lot like everyone else's. I was singing their praises and their doubts, not only my own. I was applying poetry to other people's questions. I was giving voice to their gratefulness.

We don't have to do anything to make creativity spiritual, or vice versa. Creativity already has spiritual components. And spirituality, when allowed to do its work, will lead us to creativity in every area of life. In my situation perhaps the connections were more pronounced than they are for most people: my prayers led to the creation of songs, and my songs reflected my prayers. I don't think it's a coincidence that American blues and country-western music have their roots in gospel music. Many of our best musicians started out in church choir. In part this is because church choir was the main, sometimes the only, form of music available in poor rural communities. But church is where many of us learn to express our spirit in a creative way. It's where we first understand that the Spirit moves in poetry and song. For many of us church is the first larger audience we have for our own words, spoken or sung aloud, our knees shaking as we blink back tears and try to communicate to the world who we are on the inside.

Creative work is soul work; it happens in that interior place where spiritual life forms the rest of life. Your spiritual beliefs and your creative drive reside in the same place—deep within you where everything important is stored. Doesn't matter if you call this your spirit or something else. I call it the soul, because that's nice and general and people can attach whatever meanings they want. It's that interior location where the real you lives. The real you involves your drives, your beliefs, your desires, even your reactions to the physical world. This is where your stories happen, if you're a writer. It's where your visions appear, if you're a painter. It's where your curiosity and tenacity live, if you are a scientist or inventor. The work that evolves from you begins in that very honest, private place that I call the soul. So it cannot be separated easily from those other residents of the soul, which include your collection of beliefs, religious and otherwise.

Your soul carries your wounds, and woundedness is a spiritual issue. Your soul harbors the possibilities for growth, forgiveness, honesty and true change. Often what you are working out creatively is in part an expression of what is happening in your spiritual reality. You can't pick and choose as much as you might think.

My first novel was very much an expression of my own process of leaving fundamentalist Christianity while retaining the essential beliefs that made me Christian. I could have tried to make the book something else, but my spiritual journey was located right in the center of the fictional story. All I could do was go with it and work with it. Even the second novel, written during a much less tumultuous time, gave flesh to my spiritual posture. I have realized since that Velma, the title character, is a shameless version of my own religious persona, even though I have said many times that she was modeled more on my mother than any other actual person.

This is not to say that I will have to use every work of fiction to process my religious life. But at that time I could not have separated the fiction from the religion had I tried feverishly to do so. Every artist in one way or another is expressing some aspect of his or her deeper nature. You may be expressing your questions, your anger, your celebration, your awe or your warped sense of humor, but the art will always lead back to some part of you. This is one reason that creativity is very much about spirituality. Even if you don't consider yourself a spiritual person (though I think that most people do), you are acting out of passions and reflections, thought processes and emotional attachments that are quite deep and true, and they make up your spiritual life.

⚘ THE INTERACTION OF CREATIVITY AND SPIRITUALITY

It's not accurate to talk about these two aspects of life as separate entities. Those of us in the West are journeying toward a multicultural sensibility, and we now have numerous opportunities to approach our lives holistically, whether through alternative medicine or through broader views of faith. But in day-to-day experience we often revert to a view of ourselves that is fragmented. Quite a few seasoned artists have already figured out that spirituality and creativity are closely connected. Their long years of working with creativity have taught them this, but they are ahead of most us. So as a starting point, I will talk about creativity and spirituality as though they were separate, if only to help us look at them in specific terms.

Spirituality Offers to Creativity Safety, Depth and Transcendence

Spirituality can offer a larger framework in which to place creative work. The energy and exploratory nature of creativity make it easily sidetracked and self-indulgent. Anything that is so passionate comes with its own dangers. Anything so primal and powerful needs some means of guidance and discernment. Every area of life requires appropriate boundaries. It is necessary to have checks against what can become destructive tendencies. And any aspect of the human person can become destructive. We can cite examples of religion or ambition or even good intentions turned destructive; the same is true of our sexual drive or survival drive or creative drive.

Simply put, spiritual attentiveness provides creative people with safety that they need. It's easier to go exploring when there's a base camp to which you can return. It's easier to expend huge amounts of energy when you know how to come back from that and give restoration to your mind and heart. It's easier to trust the creative process when you also trust that a greater force is somehow guiding that process. It's easier to follow a creative vision when you have a community that's giving you moral support. So whether your spirituality involves a specific religious tradition or a set of practices that give you stability, it is a great boon to your creative endeavors.

Spirituality can offer depth and direction to creative work. A well-written short story can be a real kick to read, but a well-written short story that dips into matters of the soul can be life changing. When you make a song or film whose foundation is some incredible theme such as liberation or dignity or the sacrifices made by love, that song or film offers something to the world that goes far beyond the words and images. When the characters in your novel or play are working through emotional issues, you can create a moving story; when they are working through spiritual issues, you can create a transcendent story.

Writer Philip Yancey suggests that Christianity survived in Soviet Russia because of the novels written by Leo Tolstoy and Feodor Dostoyevsky. During the decades when church was outlawed and atheism was conditioned into the masses, the spirituality of these stories reached people at a deep, intuitive level, and faith survived in a miraculous, widespread way. This is just a hint at what our creativity gains when we allow it to be infused with spirituality.

Spirituality can make creativity less bound by time, space and fashion. This is because the great spiritual themes are woven throughout history. A psychologist or anthropologist might say that the spiritual themes found in the Bible and other sacred writings derive from the archetypes and the collective wisdom of all people and all times. So if our creative work draws on these great themes, its impact will be longer lasting than that of the latest literary fad.

Creativity Offers to Spirituality Detail, Distinction and Imagination

Creativity can give to spirituality the color, form, taste and texture that bring the theoretical straight into us as real experience. Our spirits live in bodies, and those bodies respond to sensory information. Our creative gifts provide means by which to infuse our theology and philosophy with real life. Make your theme taste and sound like something, and your audience will get it.

Creativity can give to your spirituality the unique stamp that is your personality. This is the story that only you could write; it waited for you to be born and grow up and learn how to make sentences. Creativity is what makes one day different from the next. It lies in the concrete specifics of a situation or person; this is why we remember this film rather than that one. Creativity makes it possible for no two paintings or poems to be alike.

Creativity can reveal the beauty and wonder of the spiritual life. Every time you create something, you are re-creating something that God created, and you are re-creating it in such a way that for certain people it will seem like the very first time they discovered rhythm or kindness or that particular shade of yellow. Our creativity rebirths the world in all of its detail again and again. As artists we name the world and help other people recognize the grace, wisdom and wonder that have been present all along.

Creativity will wake you up to what the spiritual life is all about. Until you learn creativity, you won't really notice the details of your life with God. Creativity will sharpen your every sense, and you will be more able to hear and see all that is happening in your life. Creativity is God's way of teaching us to pay attention, to think and to dream. It adapts itself constantly by attending to details; this is why we can finally visualize how to take steps and accomplish our goals.

Creativity activates imagination, and imagination is one of our most valuable spiritual faculties. Every aspect of the spiritual life requires some imagination. When you make a leap of faith, you are imagining as real whatever faith declares as true. When you find wisdom through reading a book or hearing a story or attending a workshop, you must employ imagination in order to visualize how that wisdom can be applied to your own circumstances. When you love another person through forgiveness or a listening ear or helping hand, you must first empathize, which requires the ability to put yourself in that person's place. When you pray, you imagine the help that you need. When you make plans for the future, you construct a vision of what that future might be. When you must finally forgive yourself and move on, you can do so only by imagining a love that is bigger and more powerful than the normal sort of love of which you are capable.

You might think of the spiritual as intangible reality and of creativity as the means by which the intangible is made concrete so that you can experience it. However you think of spirituality and creativity, practice visualizing them as eternally linked.

How Do You Connect Creative Work with the Spiritual Journey?

A common approach Christians take to endow their creative work with spirituality is simply to cast it in spiritual terms—to speak of talents as "God-given gifts," to name the motivation as a "desire to glorify God," to rename the Muse as the Holy Spirit, and to attach to any creative endeavor a specific spiritual agenda, such as evangelism or at least revelation of truth. There's nothing wrong with any of these, but they touch only the surface of the process. Your engagement with the process itself needs to involve a spiritual sensibility.

One thing you can do is assume that a particular inspiration comes to you for a reason. Your spirit is speaking to you when you draw that particular poem out of your well. You can work on the poem, but you can also ask the poem, "What are you trying to tell me about myself? What are you trying to tell me about the world?" When a line drawing stirs up emotions, follow them to whatever it is you're connecting with. When your dreams become vivid, write them down and consider what your soul is trying to help you understand or celebrate or overcome. Allow the characters in your short story to speak their mind. Listen to them. You might even put yourself in a scene with them, just as an exercise.

In other words, work with your creative material as if all of it is personal. You may be producing goods that you will sell for a profit. But allow the process of creation to be a personal one. Interact with the material as if it holds a secret you need for your own life.

Starting from the opposite direction, you can allow spiritual activities to move into creative expression. I've done this when working through a Scripture passage by way of lyrics or dramatic scripts. You can start with a prayer, liturgy, hymn, Bible study or devotional material and respond through art. Most of the time this creative work will be for you alone, but the point is not to produce a work but to connect more intentionally these two aspects of your life.

You can also make your creative-spiritual process an offering to the world. In doing this, you assume that what you create can be beneficial to others. You move forward with the attitude that you have good work to do and that the universe waits for your efforts. Your posture toward the creative work becomes that of service. In a way you submit yourself to the process and the vision. You open your hands and heart, willing for the work to develop as it needs to for a greater good.

This may sound rather esoteric and idealistic, but see what happens inside you when you state your intentions in this way. You might even create a practice, or ritual, of offering your work to God or to your community or to some other entity that lies beyond your personal goals and abilities. Invite nature and the whole universe to participate with you as you create. This inner move can certainly do you no harm.

CREATIVE FORMATION

A lot of us have grown up with some idea of spiritual formation. Many types of it exist, connected to particular religious orders and faith traditions. These systems of formation operate out of certain principles, which I've generalized into the following list.

- The healthy spiritual life *is an intentional life,* in which the person examines options and opportunities, necessities and desires, and makes choices accordingly.
- The healthy spiritual life *follows a process* which deals with the whole person and in which the person participates willingly.
- The healthy spiritual life *requires community,* not only mentors and

leaders but companions who enable the person to survive the difficulties and fully appreciate the blessings.

- The healthy spiritual life *has certain goals before it*; these goals serve to motivate and encourage the person who is in the midst of the process.
- The healthy spiritual life *involves practices* that help the person engage meaningfully in the process of formation.
- The healthy spiritual life *is not only purposeful but joyful*, because the person is being formed into the creation she or he was meant to become.

Why not approach the creative life in a similar way? Let's rewrite the above principles with creativity in mind.

- *The healthy creative life is an intentional life, in which the person examines options and opportunities, necessities and desires, and makes his or her own choices accordingly.* You are able to examine your loves, gifts and dreams and make choices that are right for you and your situation.
- *The healthy creative life follows a process which deals with the whole person and in which the person participates willingly.* You have been invited to participate in a process that is bigger and wiser than you are. Your gifts can join the gifts of others in the grand scheme of creativity that operates throughout the world. This process involves every aspect of your life, and as you participate with your creative gifts, you cannot help but grow into a fuller version of who you are.
- *The healthy creative life requires community, not only mentors and leaders but companions who help the person to survive the difficulties and fully appreciate the blessings.* You are designed to give and receive. You can give out of your creative gifts, but you must also receive from others wisdom, encouragement and simple company. Sometimes you will need help in your creative journey, and sometimes your help will be called upon to assist another's journey.

- *The healthy creative life has certain goals before it; these goals serve to motivate and encourage the person who is in the midst of the process.* You are capable of envisioning your gifts as more fully developed. And this vision can help you make plans for your creative development.

- *The healthy creative life involves practices that help the person engage meaningfully in the process of formation.* You have the responsibility to develop practices that help your gifts. Only you can examine your creative needs and set out to provide for them. You have the ability to design rituals, habits and practices that help you engage more fully in your creative gifts and in the larger creative process.

- *The healthy creative life is not only purposeful but joyful, because the person is doing what she or he is gifted to do.* You have the opportunity to enter your own life more joyfully as you discover and develop your creative gifts. Your joy and your gifts are inherently linked, and it is your great privilege to discover both.

The following simple questions are designed to help you relate your life right now to these principles.

The healthy creative life is an intentional life . . .
- How intentional have I been about my creative development?
- What options are open to me now?
- What opportunities am I looking for?
- What do I perceive as necessary in order to move forward in my creative life?
- What are my desires telling me?
- What choices should I be making at this juncture?

The healthy creative life follows a process . . .
- What do I know about the process of creativity?

- What have I discovered about my personal part in that process?
- What happens to me in the course of a creative work?
- Am I open to the influence this larger process can have on every aspect of my life?
- Am I willing to go where the process takes me?

The healthy creative life requires community . . .
- How would I describe my community?
- Who participates with me in the creative life?
- Whom can I encourage, and who can encourage me?
- Where can I go when I need wisdom and instruction?
- Whom can I involve when a work is complete and ready to be shared with the world?

The healthy creative life has certain goals before it . . .
- What will my life look like when I have truly engaged with my gifts?
- What specific goals can I set before myself and work toward?
- What qualities do I want to nurture in my personality and lifestyle that will support my gifts and put them to work?

The healthy creative life involves practices . . .
- What practices have I always had that involved my creative life?
- What additional practices do I need in order to tap my creativity and work at my craft?
- What lifelong practices will help me stay engaged with the creative process in healthy ways?

The healthy creative life is not only purposeful but joyful . . .
- Do I regularly experience joy?
- Do I know what at least some of my gifts are?

- Am I doing what I'm gifted to do?
- Do my creative gifts shape my overall life purpose?

I have used these questions in shaping the chapters that follow. Each chapter explores an aspect of the artistic life and offers help as you move forward in your own creative formation.

❧ Exercises for a Writer's Formation

Once upon a Time

Choose one of the following sentences, add "and here's what happened," and write till you complete the thought:

Once upon a time, my soul woke up

Once upon a time, I met God

Once upon a time, I discovered my spiritual life

Creative-Spiritual Intersections

What do these things have to do with creativity?

truth

wisdom

compassion

generosity

renewal

healing

regeneration

discipline

exploration

What seems to happen to me spiritually when I'm in the heat of creation?

What seems to happen to my creative self when I am in the midst of spiritual awareness or joy?

Here's a description of ways in which my spirituality and creativity have seemed to fight each other.

Here are ways in which they have seemed to aid or instruct each other.

Faith Object

I am going to create an object that represents my spirituality at this time in my life. It's an object small enough to carry in my arms. I will make it a certain shape, color, size and texture. It will have its own fragrance, which I will try to describe. When I'm close to this object it makes its own sound, which I will also try to describe.

When the artist is truly the servant of the work, the work is better than the artist; Shakespeare knew how to listen to his work, and so he often wrote better than he could write; Bach composed more deeply, more truly than he knew; Rembrandt's brush put more of the human spirit on canvas than Rembrandt could comprehend.

MADELEINE L'ENGLE, *WALKING ON WATER*

A dynamic struggle goes on within a person between what he or she consciously thinks on the one hand and, on the other, some insight, some perspective that is struggling to be born. The insight is then born with anxiety, guilt, and the joy and gratification that is inseparable from the actualizing of a new idea or vision.

ROLLO MAY, *THE COURAGE TO CREATE*

Somehow the endlessly recombining elements that make up works of fiction have their roots hooked, it seems, into the universe, or at least into the hearts of human beings. Somehow the fictional dream persuades us that it's a clear, sharp, edited version of the dream all around us.

JOHN GARDNER, *THE ART OF FICTION*

The amount of matter in the universe is limited. . . . But no such limitation of numbers applies to the creation of works of art. The poet is not obliged, as it were, to destroy the material of a Hamlet in order to create a Falstaff, as a carpenter must destroy a tree-form to create a table-form. The components of the material world are fixed; those of the world of imagination increase by a continuous and irreversible process, without any destruction or rearrangement of what went before.

DOROTHY SAYERS, *THE MIND OF THE MAKER*

3 THE PRACTICES THAT ENGAGE THE PROCESS

*What It Means to Participate
with Mystery and Muse*

When I received the contract for my first novel, my situation was fairly impossible for novel writing. I was in my first job since grad school, as an assistant editor in a very small publishing company. I'd been married about a year and was living in the city while working thirty-some miles away. This required a commute that involved car and train and took four to five hours from my day. My husband recently had been waylaid by a clinical depression and was unemployed. Given my beginner's salary, this meant that I was not only editing full time but taking all the freelance proofreading and typing jobs I could find. I left home at 6:00 a.m. and never returned earlier than 7:00 p.m. And by that time I was too spent to even consider sitting at my desk and clocking another hour or two at my computer, writing amazing fiction.

There was, however, the train commute, about fifty minutes one way. And I did have a laptop, a used one that had its irritating little habits but worked more or less. If I was going to get the novel written, I would have to haul the laptop with me and use the train time.

Allowing time for startup and shutdown, I could safely write for half an hour or forty minutes and still pull myself together to exit the train with my coat buttoned and all my stuff packed. But what could I do in thirty minutes?

Not only that, but I had been riding the same train car at the same time most mornings for a year, and half the people on it were now friends of mine. We spent the entire ride catching up with one another's business and reading the paper, often aloud and with group commentary. How would I actually write in this space?

But it was my very first contract, and I couldn't screw it up. Finally I had the opportunity to publish a novel. I didn't imagine it would come close to the magic of *To Kill a Mockingbird,* but I owed this opportunity everything I could give it.

Well, I explained to my train community that some days I would need to work and to please not take personally my withdrawal from the conversation. (As I recall, I did not say that I was writing a novel; that would have sounded too pretentious. They knew that I did editorial work, so they would just assume that was what I was doing.) They were fine with this announcement, and whenever I took out the laptop and sat one seat back from my usual spot, they respected my need to be left alone.

And I decided that I would just open the laptop and type and hope that something good happened. I didn't expect to feel inspired precisely between 7:00 and 7:30 a.m. or between 6:30 and 7:00 p.m. Inspiration at that point was a luxury. So my writing life was not luxurious. For a beginning novelist, luxury is a lot to expect anyway.

I wrote a lot of decent prose on that train. And when the book was published, I handed out copies. It was special to me because I'd done what felt impossible. It was special to my train buddies when they realized that this published, real book had been written in their presence.

We often speak of creativity as something that acts upon us. Or it is an entity, and we are simply at its mercy. We wait for inspiration to strike. We hope for the right idea to come. We long for the energy it takes to write that chapter. We tend to take on the role of a passive vessel, waiting to be filled.

This viewpoint is rather romantic—and dramatic. It paints the creative person as a lover desperately awaiting the beloved's reciprocation. Unfortunately, this view of creativity does not result in much creative work actually happening. It results mostly in waiting and frustration and finally resignation.

Artists have long spoken of "the Muse," inspiration personified. According to *Webster's*, the Muse was "any of the nine sister goddesses in Greek mythology presiding over song and poetry and the arts and sciences." Well, you are not at the mercy of the Muse. Repeat this statement to yourself until you believe it. You are not an artist who is unable to work until Miss Muse appears with her charms. You are not an empty vessel waiting to be filled or an instrument in God's hand waiting for the hand to do something.

You are a *participant*. Even when God performed miracles out in the Old Testament wilderness, God required that some human being *do* something, such as talk to a stubborn pharaoh or pick up a staff and start walking. Even when we are waiting for further instruction or for an idea to form more clearly, we are active in some way. Creative work requires that we do something, and keep doing it. It's the doing that brings the real results.

As a writer I know that nothing really happens until I write. Now I may write for hours or days before what I write turns into anything meaningful. But I have to write for all those hours in order to arrive at *the* hour in which the "inspired" writing happens.

If you want to cast this in more clearly spiritual terms, then consider that part of what you do in order to create is to submit. As a participant, you are submitting to a divine process that is beyond you. If you are a person of religious faith, then you participate and submit out of faith in the One who watches over the process and your involvement in it.

CREATIVE WORK AS AN EVENT AND A PARTNERSHIP

I like to think of creativity as a celestial drama in which each of us walks on and off stage at various points. It's a huge show with trillions of acts, big and small, scaling the centuries and cultures, informing humanity constantly and at multiple levels. You and I dip into the action as we respond to the smaller dramas in our own soul. We answer single soft voices, never knowing where our individual efforts fall within the overarching story line.

When we delve into our creativity, we are responding to something that's bigger than us. It may call to us from a personal place and in specific language, but that is the individual soul chiming in with the larger spiritual calling. Whether we like it or not, we are connected to the world with all its people, its needs and ideas, and our creativity is one form of that connection. Shakespeare and Ansel Adams may have been operating out of entirely different worlds and engaging in their art for entirely different reasons, but each was giving the world something it needed and something it was calling for at that particular time.

When you respond to your creative calling, you are doing something that is necessary for the world. It may be necessary in big ways—say a series of newspaper articles that can help shape the consciousness of a generation. Or it may be necessary in small ways—perhaps a charcoal sketch that brings you, the artist, healing. But art is not a luxury. Creative works are called out by cultural and personal needs that are too deep and intuitive to be obvious every time. We know, for instance, that music helps us in ways that we can't always describe. Poetry and patchwork quilts are also appealing to us at an almost subconscious level. It's difficult to quantify such quality. It would be impossible to do a spreadsheet analysis of how artistic work helps us.

Any creative work, "artistic" or not, is coming from a deeper place and answering deeper needs that cannot be named easily. In this respect we have to have faith—faith that what we do, whether an arrangement of flowers or a mathematical proof, is worth our best energy.

And so sculpture in a public park does mean something. We can only hope that the sculptor was paying close attention and producing the very image we needed. It's not a good thing when artists create without passion or any deep connection to their work. Only by attending to their creative intuition do they bring about the work they have been summoned to create.

You are called to a work, and you respond with your particular gifts, vision and energy. You're rarely sure of what it is you're about to do, but you have an idea, along with the desire to carry it out. You say yes and then hope that your skill will live up to the yes. You feel honored but maybe a bit scared too.

I think that people who participate in a creative ensemble are given a clearer picture of how creativity works in general. If you are part of a drama company, a small jazz band, a dance troupe or even an editorial department, you observe all the time how a creative call can bring together separate talents to invent something that is much greater than the sum of its parts. You know how it works, yet you are always amazed at just how well it works. You see the chemistry bubble between cast members so that it touches the audience; you watch an art show fall into place. You hear the voices blend and watch the backs bend and legs arch like poetry, and it's very clear that something large and wonderful is happening in spite of you and yet because of you.

If you've ever participated in such group efforts, remember them as you begin a project on your own. Just assume that there are other voices, images and phrases joining your own work, somewhere and somehow. Assume that whatever you do will rhyme with what others are doing and will do, or with what others have already done. In someone's life your turn of phrase will make a difference, simply because it follows another turn of phrase by another writer at another key point in this person's life. We're all on a continuum. Our creative work is on a continuum. This participation in the larger event lends even more power to our individual achievements.

One advantage of this kind of thinking is that it helps us let go of envy and jealousy. In the cosmic economy there is room for every gift. There is reason for every creative work. And every creative work enhances, and is enhanced by, the work of others. You are not alone. You are not overly important, and you are not insignificant.

It also helps us relax a little, because we realize that everything isn't up to us. I may be responding to my own creative call, but in doing so I am participating in a much larger process that has been going on and will continue after I'm gone. It will keep going whether or not I contribute to it. And if I do participate by adding my short story or recipe for pumpkin soup, then all the better.

There is a larger process, and when I tap into that, I have access to energy and wisdom beyond my own. I may work in the silence of my writing studio, but I am certainly not alone. My success, although it depends to some extent on my own hard work, is also supported by that larger framework of creativity that's happening throughout the world. It's not all in my lap. If this particular creative venture goes well, that's good, but if it turns out to be little more than a good exercise, the world is no worse for it.

At this juncture it helps to remember that creative work is worthy whether it's paid work or not. The fact that creative work is entangled in the world of commerce shouldn't ruin your artistic life. You have to be pragmatic about the money part. If you make a good living at your work, that's wonderful. But you can't dismiss the work that doesn't bring you money. I never made a dime off the one hundred-plus songs I spent nearly two decades writing, and I'll never be known for them. But they did a certain work at a certain time. It was work that I needed to do and others were glad I did.

Creative work is also worthy whether or not it has an audience. Much of the work you do will be more for your personal development than for anyone else's needs. Your task is to engage in the work you are called to do. I've written a dozen or more short stories, several of them very meaningful to me. One of them was published several years ago; the rest are in a file that I return to from time to time, but I have no hopes of selling them, and I rarely share them with anyone else. I don't think those stories are really good enough for an audience, but they were good enough for me when I wrote them. They helped my writing progress, and they satisfied something for me personally, and that's enough.

Feel free to pursue the audience and the money. But don't entangle your creative life with the consumer culture. The point is the work itself, not how "marketable" it is. Your first reason for doing it is simply that it calls to be done.

That larger Creativity calls, then, and you're pretty sure that you heard your name. Don't be shy about it. Get happy. You have work to do. You have something to contribute. It's not up to you to decide how much or how important. The question is: do you dare participate in something so beyond you, something that communicates to the larger world and is also influenced by that world?

Although I've spoken in terms of what the person gives to the world through her creativity, I don't want to leave the impression that the gift giving is one-sided. As you participate in the creative process, that process will, quite frankly, work you over. It will teach you about yourself. It will perform therapy on you. It will heal you. You are called to a process that you actually need for your own well-being. And you don't give the world any gift that you don't first partake of yourself. You, after all, are the very first audience for the work you are creating. You're the first to visualize that stunning scene, to hear that particular harmony. You're the first to "get it." Did you ever think about that? Every creative work you produce you also witness. You are the first witness. When you witness creative power and wisdom, your life will be changed; it's inevitable.

Don't forget that while you participate in creativity for what you can give to the world, you also participate because you need to. This is the way it is supposed to work.

CREATIVE PROCESS AS BOTH INDIVIDUAL AND UNIVERSAL

Creative work is often solitary work. It requires a lot of time with one's soul. It requires reflection, work and then more reflection, and much of this happens when the artist is alone. And even when an artist is out with friends or going about other business, there is often that other self that keeps musing on the work in progress.

It takes confidence in yourself as a creative person to make the time and space needed for your process to work itself out. Your creative process is as individual as you are. And while you can talk to other creatives and learn from them, in the end you must settle for yourself what your process actually is and what you must do to facilitate it.

This means that, deep down, you have to believe that there is a process and that this process is yours to own. You have to be willing to take a stand and put boundaries around your time and energy. When people ask what you're doing, you can give them an answer or not, but you must know for yourself what that answer is.

You can begin to understand the creative process by exploring some aspects of it that are generally the same for everyone. When creative people talk with each other and reveal aspects of their individual processes, they nearly always find certain traits and phases in common. As they communicate with one another, they can piece together a rough sketch of how creativity works and thus become more comfortable with it, more confident in working with it. Once you identify parts of the process for yourself, you can attend to the more individual traits of your own work.

The Beginning: Visions and Chaos

The beginning of a creative work is often quite dramatic. People speak of having an "aha!" experience, of seeing a film's character clearly and knowing what's going to happen to her or him. Or there's a sort of vision of what the final work might look like or sound like. For some, a single line reveals an entire poem to come, or a title sets them on a journey to find the novel. My nephew is a painter, and he actually has visions of completed works before he begins painting them.

The senses are stimulated, the adrenaline is triggered. Some people enter a happy, giddy phase, so full of energy that they can't get to work fast enough. For others, it's a slow dawning and a growing excitement.

For some people, the beginning is a time of complete chaos. You see bits and pieces of what is before you. You have a sense of what it is you must set out to do. But nothing will form yet. When you sit down to write or paint or form movement, it's like stepping over a cliff or into a dense fog. All you can do is trust that this impending masterpiece is going to somehow manifest itself as you work. But you do know that there is something specific ahead, and you feel the excitement of that.

For those of us who process life in a more left-brained way, the beginning of a work may consist of a series of lists and diagrams. I know one writer who begins a book by composing a table of contents. It doesn't matter that the table of contents will likely change as the book is being written; this person must organize first. I begin most nonfiction that way, whereas my fiction's beginning is often less formed.

The point is, each of us has a way of beginning. There are things we do that get the process going. Each person must figure out what actions work for him or her.

Let's talk about emotions. Just a few of the emotions that people name for this beginning phase are happiness, joy, anticipation, fear, anxiety and tension. There may be joy because of the wonderful work you imagine, but that is followed directly by fear that you won't be able to execute it well.

For me, the emotions of the beginning are similar to the infatuation that starts a romantic relationship. When you're first in love with someone, the intensity of the emotion helps you jump into relationship regardless of any dangers, probable and otherwise. You're too excited to stop and analyze or to be slowed down by fear. Sometimes you leap right over common sense too. If most of us knew how hard the relationship would turn out to be, we'd never make that first leap. But in the long term we're usually glad we did.

So you've never created a work quite like the one you're now imagining. You glance ahead and imagine, fleetingly, the difficulties: the inherent problems with this mix of characters or the long hours of research that will be required. But this is such a great idea! You're going to try it regardless of everything. This is the type of enthusiasm that helps launch many creative works.

Physically, this can be a time of great energy, of increased joy and enthusiasm. Some people experience just the opposite, a sudden drop in energy as if the whole body is gearing up for the work at hand. Others experience sleep disturbances; they lie awake trying to get their mind around the work.

The excitement of the beginning can tempt us to talk about the upcoming project. Some talk is helpful, especially if you're the type of person who processes a lot of your thinking out loud. For some of us, though, speaking ideas aloud can impede those ideas' formation. We must beware of talking so much about a project that we waste the energy that should go to working on it. Each person has to understand when talking is good for the process and when it's not.

The Middle: Struggle and Engagement

The middle of the creative process is generally the longest period, because that's when most of the work happens. It may happen quickly, in a few days or weeks. Or it may drag on for months or even years, as the artist struggles to work out the vision. The middle is a time of engagement, when the person becomes absorbed in the work. This is when your craft comes into play, because by this time you have a clearer idea of what you're doing—the hard part is doing it well. So after the first flush of working out a story, you understand better what must happen and when, but the real work is to flesh it out in the way that works best. For me as a writer that means dealing with viewpoint, scenes, tension, characterization. The middle of a creative work involves a lot of reworking.

For some people, the middle feels similar to a depression, because you don't yet see the end. You're not at all sure there *is* an end. Some days you feel that you've taken yourself on a wild chase that's brought you to a vacant lot where you expected to find a majestic cathedral or at least a pretty patch of flowers. You're in the middle of a novel that some time ago you had a clear vision of, but it's all over the place now, and you're not sure anymore that you can write it. Or you've done what seemed right with this sculpture or orchestration, but you're not satisfied; it's not quite right—and you just don't know what to do to make it right.

At the same time, the middle—that time of full engagement—can be the most satisfying time, because you are working hard at what you are gifted to do and what you're meant to do. Some artists enjoy this middle portion more than the beginning or the end, because they can take their time, have fun with the material and get lost in the process, whereas the chaos of the beginning or the finality of the end isn't as satisfying.

The middle of the process is hard work, and it's emotionally taxing. You may lose the initial thrill and excitement, and all you're left with is an overwhelming mess that you're not even sure you like anymore. The middle is often the point at which you discover the gaps in your own abilities, as you rework and rework and still that initial vision won't become reality.

Sometimes a person quits in the middle. It's tough going, and unless you're truly committed to the work, it's easier to let it go and start something else. By this time you are so ready for a new adrenaline rush, a new vision with its burst of energy. It's tempting to start a new project when you're splat in the middle of one that is requiring hard work.

That horrible middle is one reason that some of us have more than one project going at once. One day I get out of bed and just cannot face that hairy, unwieldy novel. So I let it rest for a day or even a week, and I turn to another project, usually nonfiction. The danger is that I will get sidetracked from the novel altogether, long enough that I lose my nerve to return to it. But it's good not to feel trapped by one and only one work. Opinions vary on this, but my thought is that sometimes you do need to rest from a project. And it's nearly always better to rest from a single project than to rest from creative work altogether. So I am working on essays for a few days—at least I'm writing, putting words together, crafting sentences and bringing ideas to life. To me that's better than not writing at all.

Creative work is multifaceted enough that it's possible to find rest within it by shifting tasks. Maybe I can't face the really right-brained creative work today, so this is a perfect time to go back to another section and do some rigorous editing. Switching back and forth between various tasks is perfectly fine for that long middle phase. Every now and then you really need to stop and do some research—maybe go to a gallery and absorb someone else's paintings that are in the same medium you're using or that deal with a similar subject. So your creative work for today is to go and gaze.

As you become more familiar with your own ebbs and flows, you'll learn to relax and recognize the many different faces and phases of your work. Within a creative life there is actually much variety, and this can make those long periods of engagement a little easier to get through.

The End: Closure and Release

For some people, the finishing of a work is deeply gratifying and grounds for a triple-chocolate dessert. For others it's a time of sadness and depression, as a project in which they've been deeply invested comes to an end. And for many of us this is a fearful time, because once we've finished the work we must put it out there and see what others will make of it. For the novelist, it's the fear of waiting for book reviews and sales figures. Each creative realm has its form of judgment, and often this is one of the first things we face when we have declared, "It's finished." After the work is completed, it must be released, and that is so difficult that sometimes the release never quite happens.

The end is difficult in that you must make a decision. You must ask yourself, *Is this the best I can do? Is this really finished now?* Those are two frightening questions. The truth is, you will never know for sure when you've done your best. Some pieces could keep evolving for years. But at some point you as the creator need closure.

It's a disappointment to come to the end of a project and realize that it doesn't live up to what you had imagined. I have a little saying that I give to writers and have to repeat to myself often: *Your vision will always exceed your abilities.* We need to come to terms with this truth. Thank God that our visions are always beyond us; this is how we grow as artists. But that makes it hard to finally close up work on a piece, because we can nearly always imagine it just a notch better, one level up from where it is now.

Sometimes a work contains a flaw that cannot be undone unless the entire work is undone, and you have to decide that it's not worth the destruction to deal with that foundational flaw. And so you have to admit to yourself that it's a flawed piece—and let it go.

Sometimes you have done all you can do for now. And you let it go, put it away, and then—who knows? Years later you may pick it up and with advanced abilities and wisdom be able to re-create the work so that it is finally ready for an audience.

You must be willing to close up shop. You must be willing to say that you're not perfect and that you've not lived up to your own expectations. At that point there's nothing to do but be grateful for the work you've been able to do and celebrate all that you learned in the process. Any work increases your skill, even if the work itself is never quite good enough to suit you.

Another reason the end of the process can be difficult is that you are then faced with finding another beginning. You may have other projects waiting in the wings. But if a project has consumed your life for quite a while, it can be scary to face the void once it is finished.

Many artists find that they need to take a break and rest before embarking on a new project. Even if they have projects waiting, something within keeps them from diving into something new right away. It may require a break of a day or a couple of weeks, but the mental and emotional rest feels necessary. Others find that they can readily dip into the next thing fairly soon after they've finished a project. The important thing is to be aware of what you need.

Another aspect of endings is that so often they are not what we had envisioned. I thought this person in the story would die, but as it turned out, someone else did. Or I had hoped the girl would get the guy, but that's not the way the story spun itself. Or I thought this was a novel about redemption, but as the characters have told their tales, the real theme has become something else entirely. The end of a project is often one more proof that I am not—and have never been—in control of this creation.

This can be particularly irritating when you're creating in order to fulfill a contract. I had to find an agent who would get me out of one book contract, because the novel I had thought would fit within a certain genre and suit a certain audience was flailing outside both boundaries. I couldn't in good conscience force the story to become something else, but I knew that once in the hands of this particular publisher, drastic changes would be demanded. I wasn't willing to get into that fight. The lesson I took from this: don't contract for a novel that isn't finished yet.

Talk with other creative folks and compare notes about your processes. You will find some things in common, and you'll learn some new angles on the creative life. You may be encouraged by listening to how someone else made it through that long middle phase. You may gain wisdom about how to decide when you've done all you can do and can finish the work at hand.

CREATIVE PROCESS AS A FIELD FOR EXPLORATION

The creative genius will likely never be understood completely, but our creativity will give us clues if we learn to be attentive. If we pay attention to our process, we will be better able to do our work skillfully and more confidently.

We give creativity a lot of power because it is so mysterious to us. Most artists live with a deep fear that the Muse may or may not show up. I still sit down to write some days and this little voice says, "What if it doesn't happen today? What if you never again have anything to write? What if not one sentence works out, if you can't really finish this book?" Experienced artists probably fear it as well, but they have worked long enough to understand how the work really happens. They've built habits and learned discipline. And they have discovered that much of what they do is a matter of practice, of developing a craft, and that they can do that, Muse or no Muse.

But if you are not very experienced at really working with your gifts, you will allow them to become mysterious beings that you must obey. For instance, if I know from experience that inspiration arrives under certain conditions, I will make sure to re-create the conditions that invited it initially. Thus my early experience comes to determine how it is I will work. Isn't it odd that when it comes to creativity we are quite reluctant to be creative? We think we cannot function unless the kids are out of the house or we're at some exotic location or we've finished sorting out the hall closet. We can't imagine the flexibility in our creativity that the creativity itself reveals to be operating in everything else.

I did my pilot workshop on creativity and spirituality at the Community of Jesus on Cape Cod. Three of the participants, all artists, were members of the community's monastic order. One sister brought up the problem of time and environment. Visiting artists often came to the community, she said, to help with music or plays or visual arts. One particular artist would stay up all night to do the work. That's the way he worked; he'd get into the flow and just keep going.

"But I'm in a religious order, and my day follows a set pattern. I can't stay up all night. My calling as a sister doesn't allow me erratic schedules. Does that mean I can't be as creative as that artist?"

What a good question. I suggested that the artist who stayed up all night had discovered that it worked for him. But that didn't mean that he couldn't work any other way; he had just never had to figure out another way. Would God call a person to belong to a monastic order that kept a set schedule and yet give her a creative gift that would operate only outside the schedule? I believe creativity is much more flexible than that. Our problem is that we're afraid to mess with it too much. We're afraid to make our own demands on it.

It is possible to figure out what you need in order to do your work. You can learn to recognize how you generally react to the beginning, middle and end of your process. You can figure out what the nonnegotiables are. You may need a certain amount of meditation time before you can begin a work session. Does it have to be meditation time in the woods, or in a pinch can a bathroom with a locked door and a bubble bath suffice? You may need a longer uninterrupted period to do massive rewriting. Does that have to be at a certain time and location, or can you rearrange basic components of your schedule at home?

Be reasonable about the amount of company you need and when. At some point you may need to put the work away and go have fun for a while. You may need to talk with other writers about something that's got you stuck, or you may need to reread the section on viewpoint in a helpful book. Sometimes you're not doing the actual work but other tasks that support the work. Learn when and how, and then do those support tasks without guilt or apology.

It's important that you learn what happens to you emotionally during your process. If you know that you get anxious or disgusted or blue at a certain point nearly every time, then just expect it, and when you enter that period you can say to yourself, *Okay, I'm in my funky time. I'll ride it out and finish this just as I did the last time.* If there are certain supports that help during that time, you can get them lined up. You can learn, at least to some extent, what kind of help you can get for yourself and what's not helpful. Maybe you need to stay away from crowds or avoid reading other writers you admire. Maybe you need a better diet and more sleep during this period of deep engagement—or maybe you work best while eating light and taking naps.

I enter a mild depression in the middle of every book I write (or edit, for that matter). I'm in too deep to back out, yet I cannot see the end and I'm just not excited anymore. Because I know this about myself, I now take this depressive period as a good sign; it means I'm halfway finished! I don't worry about it or try to ease it; I simply keep going, because I know that I'll work through it in a while.

You can also figure out what kind of feedback you need and when. Learn when a thorough critique is helpful and when it's poison. Learn when to ask for advice and when you simply need encouragement—these are two very different types of help. Sometimes your ego is more fragile than others. You're the only person who can name your moods and needs.

Many variables will affect how your process works itself out. Are you an introvert or extravert? Do you work best with a deadline, or do deadlines make you choke up? Are you able to approach works as projects that require plans, or is creativity more undefined for you? What disruptions bother you more—physical irritations and discomforts or emotional upsets in the atmosphere around you? Your process will not look exactly like anyone else's. At the same time, you'll be surprised at how many people struggle with similar issues. It can only help to share stories and information.

There will always be mystery in the creative process, and we would be disappointed if it became a science we could sketch out in detail. Discovery is half the fun. But you can learn a lot about how the process works for you—and then work with it.

Most of all, you can keep in mind that, although the creative drive has a life of its own, it is not the boss of you. It is part of you, and you can learn to get along without either of you being compromised. Mature artists learn eventually that their creativity seems to thrive within certain patterns and environments, but it will still work in other pat-

terns and environments. Say your ideal environment is long blocks of
time to yourself, out in the woods without kids and maybe even without your significant other. Your real life is not like this. Your family is
more important than this creative project. The creative project, after
all, is something that comes from you, a product of sorts; your partner
and kids are other human beings to whom you have made a commitment. So you will carve out a few times in a year when everyone is out
of your hair and you can be near the woods. But the rest of the time
you will juggle all your loves, some days more successfully than others. The work will still get done. The process may not be so dramatic
with people yammering around you, but there's no point in being attached to the drama. It's fun, but it's not the main thing.

～ CREATIVE PRACTICES AS A WAY OF LIFE

A good life doesn't just happen. And creative gifts don't emerge fully
developed. As a book editor of twelve years, I am well acquainted with
the *unpracticed* art of word crafting. Most people would never dream
of picking up a flute, learning a few scales and a tune or two, and pro-
ceeding to put on a concert and charge money for it. We are aware of
all that we don't know about music—the technique, the theory, the experience. Yet because most of us know English well enough to communicate through conversation, we assume that it's only a little jump
from there to writing a coherent book.

Good writers practice and study and practice some more. They may
not call it practice—they may simply keep writing, day after day—but
in fact they are practicing every time they write. Good writers figure
out what they need to do to develop their raw gifts into sentences and
paragraphs that will move readers.

You already have numerous practices. If you are like most Americans, you drink caffeine in the morning before you try to think too
much. This is a practice. You may have learned to do some stretches
in the morning or evening in order to relieve physical stress. This is a
practice.

I light a little oil lamp before I start my writing time. This sets aside the next couple of hours as sacred time, for I consider that when I work at my gifts I am doing holy work. These are gifts God gave me, and I want to use them for good on this earth. So I light my lamp and settle into a time of holy engagement. This lamp lighting is a practice.

I won't provide many definitions in this book, but here's one: *A practice is an act that helps you to engage with the process.*

The process is indeed mysterious and outside of your control. But you engage with that mysterious process by way of practices. Practices enable to you become a master of your craft, and that mastery is the control you do have and for which you are responsible. I am doing my best not to preach, but here's a one-sentence sermon that I may deliver more than once: You cannot control the process, but you must master your craft.

A professional basketball player has a plan for his work. He has warm-up exercises as well as practices that strengthen him for specific movements. Over time he learns what he can and cannot eat and drink before a game. Perhaps he takes vitamins or herbal supplements, or he spends regular time in prayer or meditation. But he is working at his game all the time, cataloging what helps and what hinders, and the actions that help he turns into practices.

This is what you must do for your creative life. You must learn what inspires you and what puts a serious cramp in your creative flow. You must learn how your body reacts to different times of the day, to certain foods, to caffeine or alcohol. It's up to you to keep track of what works and doesn't work—and then turn what works into practices.

I've learned that I can write any time of the day, but I'm usually better off if I do the bulk of my writing early in the day or at the end of the day, when other tasks aren't pulling at me so much. I've learned that a glass of wine is sometimes good for me before the evening meal or when I'm in social situations, such as visiting with neighbors on the porch. But alcohol of any sort hinders my writing (what it hinders is my judgment, making me think I am the greatest humorist who ever touched a keypad), and I avoid it when I've got work to do. I've learned that caffeine—in the form of strong black tea or a cappuccino—will stimulate my energy and help me ignore my own resistance to creative work. So I save most of my tea drinking for writing time. Cappuccino or other espresso drinks I reserve for when I'm talking with writer friends, because my ideas seem to multiply when those two ingredients—talking with friends and drinking espresso—are combined.

You have almost unlimited possibilities when it comes to forming practices that serve your creative life. They fall into a few general categories.

Some Practices Are Linked to Your Process

You will find that some practices enhance certain stages of your process. I know that putting on baroque music and brewing a pot of tea helps me settle down and write. Unless circumstances prevent those practices, I make them part of my writing day. Some people light a candle, say a prayer or do stretches as a prelude to creative work. Some people religiously follow some practice for beginning; they need that bit of preparation in order to get into the flow. For instance, some writers begin by reading what they wrote the day before; that primes the pump for the present day. Others begin by doing a writing exercise or two—something that is unrelated to the actual project but that taps the creative flow. One person I know begins by loading the dishwasher.

The beginning phase of most of my works involves walking. I'm fortunate to live about a mile from Lake Michigan, and when a new idea takes hold, I take a journal and go walking. I hardly ever write in the journal, and I don't even think that hard about the writing idea while I'm in motion. But it's percolating somewhere as I take steps and gaze at the water. I may spend an hour or an afternoon doing that.

However, once I'm into the writing itself, such walking is more distracting than anything else. I walk pretty regularly anyway, but once

I'm out of the early stage I don't walk during my writing time. At that point the walking just keeps me from the work.

It can be helpful to have a checklist, particularly once you're in the middle, most engaged stage of the work. The middle is often a muddle, and if you have some simple list of things to do or to check, that can help you keep moving. For instance, if you're stuck in the middle stage of a short story, go back to one of your basic guides for short story writing. Go through the aspects of the craft—viewpoint, character, description and so forth. Use the guide to help you step back from the work and run a basic check on it. For me, working on a novel's timeline can help me get unstuck. I spend an afternoon with a large sketchpad, outlining what happens when. That nearly always opens up the process for me in a fresh way.

So it can be helpful to have your own guide or checklist for technique and incorporate a "check" as a practice. Some people don't need a technical check as much as an inspirational check—and so they often return to other writers or works that energize them. If it helps you during the creation of a new tapestry to read the poetry of Yeats, then add that to your bag of practices.

And when you reach the end of a work, fashion some healthy practices for saying, "It's done," for letting it go and celebrating the ending. One friend of mine signals the end of a manuscript by printing it out and sending a hard copy to someone, usually her editor. It would be easier to send an electronic file, but the physical packing of the manuscript and the journey to the post office tells her, the writer, that she's letting go of it now.

The practices you use are entirely up to you. You can create as many practices as are helpful: the more the better. The only danger is that the practices replace the creative work. So you choose practices that enhance and energize the work rather than distract from it. This is why I listen to baroque music rather than some other style or genre; the passionate yet very mathematic genius of Bach or Telemann provides a background that is emotionally stimulating yet methodical and nonobtrusive. When I'm writing I generally avoid putting on sung music with words, though, because I am working on my own words.

Similarly, I alter my reading practices according to what I'm writing. I usually don't read works that are much like what I'm writing. I don't want the fiction voice of a favorite novelist to intrude on the voice I am trying to create in my own novel. Sometimes I don't read much fiction at all while I am writing fiction. And I stay away from good memoirists and creative nonfiction writers when I'm teasing out my own essays. My goal is to be well read in both fiction and nonfiction, but I practice reading in a certain way so that my writing will be enhanced, not impeded. Another writer may need to read good novels while writing her own. Each of us must find the practices that serve us best.

Some Practices Don't Appear to Be Practices

Pay attention to what you already do on a fairly regular basis. Chances are you already have practices even if you haven't yet recognized them as such. Trust your instincts, and don't be afraid of what simply makes you comfortable.

During one workshop, when we were discussing the beginning phase of creativity, one woman said with some disgust, "Well, the first thing I do is procrastinate. I'll clean out the refrigerator before I go sit down to write."

"Do you write after you clean out the refrigerator?" I asked.

"Yes."

"I think you're putting a negative spin on something that's just part of your process. You are putting order to your world before you begin. Why not just accept that as how you get ready to write?" This seemed surprising to her, but I could practically see the burden lift from her psyche. I added that sometimes before I embark on a project that requires a very free-flowing creative stage, I will clean the house or sort something. Such an ordering of my little universe seems to get me ready to hang out with the less orderly part of my brain.

What activities seem to accompany your creative work? What practices just naturally fall into your process? If you find yourself performing some act with regularity, and it's not disrupting your creativity, then label that act as a practice and don't fight it.

Some Practices Especially Nurture Creativity

Julia Cameron's *The Artist's Way* offers a lot of good ideas for stimulating creativity. One of the most helpful for me is the artist's date: once a week doing something for and with yourself that feeds your creative side. It should be fun, and it should be good for your creativity; beyond that there are no rules. I don't always keep a weekly date, but I use the artist's date as an excuse to make regular trips to downtown Chicago—a bus ride for me—and wander museums, galleries or offbeat shops that make me stop and experience others' creativity. Sometimes I take myself to a movie matinee, or I shop for a book and then go to lunch. Sometimes I simply spend extra time reading what I really like, or I rent a movie that offers inspiration or information concerning the work I'm writing. For instance, the atmosphere created in *Fried Green Tomatoes* gives me a creative boost when I write fiction set in a rural locale. Sometimes my date involves a thermos of tea and a leisurely walk along the lakefront. Nature is good for my soul, and during the warmer months I make dates to spend time in nearby parks and beside lagoons.

Feed your soul with all sorts of beauty, wonder and intrigue. Invite puzzles that challenge you, works of art that stretch you and events that charge you up. Make such fun and inspiration a regular practice. And don't feel obligated to do it alone. Some of my artist's dates are lunches out with friends who are also doing creative work. It can be twice as fun to visit the Art Institute with someone else. Some of my artist's dates include my husband or, in the case of lakefront walks, my dog.

Try stimulating other aspects of creativity. I'm not gifted in visual arts such as drawing or photography. But a year ago I took my own advice and pondered activities I really enjoyed as a child. I used to color for hours, and my parents bought me nice color-by-number books that called for a wide spectrum of colors. Remembering that, I decided to forget that I couldn't draw worth a darn, and I bought some good colored pencils and a coloring book, a collection of mandala patterns. I began to color in the evenings, often when the television was on and Jim and I were relaxing from the workday.

This diversion has provided relaxation and pleasure unlike anything I've experienced through reading or walking or watching movies. I'm learning a few things about colors. I'm beginning to get adventurous and actually mix colors. Probably my next step will be to try different strokes, such as hash marks or dots. I haven't necessarily uncovered any talent, but my creativity has been tapped in a new way, and that's been very helpful. Best of all, I can relax and just have fun, because I've got nothing to prove. Coloring has merely become one more practice for inspiring me.

Some Practices Are Habits of the Spirit

Prayer and other spiritual disciplines can help creativity simply because they are helping the interior life stay healthy.

You can look inside your own religious tradition for clues, or for something fresh and challenging, you can seek something outside your tradition. Many artists use meditation as a creative practice. Others pray in fairly traditional ways. For some, meditations on sacred writings have a regular part in their creative schedule.

If you grew up working in a conscious way with your spirituality, then you may have a practice or two that you know is good for your soul. If something works, then use it. If you have cared for your soul through a particular spiritual activity, then keep it up as you do your creative work.

You might look to devotional writings in a given tradition. Look to the artists of your own faith tradition. I am beginning to read more of the Christian mystics, because many of them tapped their creative core through certain practices, and I might learn something from them.

Look to monastic practices. Perhaps your creative life will bloom when you engage in a regular schedule of prayer or meditations on the Psalms or Gospels. Perhaps the "centering prayer" of the Quaker tradition is what you need in order to begin your creative work of the day.

Turn to the spiritual practices that have helped you in other aspects of your life. In Ignatian spirituality, the daily examen provides a way to take stock and refocus three times a day. Could you use some form of this practice to refocus your creative work? Might praying the rosary form a foundation on which to build your creative life? Could you reword the Lord's Prayer so that it relates specifically to your writing or painting? Can you use a traditional blessing or adapt it for your work? There's no end to the possibilities once you start exploring spiritual traditions.

Sometimes if I'm working with a group that is specifically Christian, toward the end of the workshop I create a service during which we bless one another's gifts. Some spiritual practices for your creativity can certainly involve other people. Some of us need others to be involved in our spiritual practices, even if that involvement is nothing more than praying for one another and our creative endeavors at specific times.

Create as many practices as you can, because sometimes they work and sometimes they don't. Their effectiveness will vary. When one thing doesn't help so much, go to something else. Experiment with a different location or different lighting. Do your work in a more structured way or a more free-flowing way. Come up with a set of practices for a certain period, and then shift to another set. I find myself adapting practices according to the season of the year. I interact with summer early morning in a much different way from how I approach 5:00 a.m. in January. And sometimes in the summer I write late at night: the weather allows me to work out on the porch, and even in the city nighttime brings a certain calm. Darkness in seventy- or eighty-degree weather can be quite soft and serene.

As noted above, brewing a pot of tea has long been part of my writing time. I don't drink coffee or soft drinks with any regularity, but I grew up drinking tea daily with my grandmother. It was not only a physical habit but a deeply ingrained emotional one. However, one of my creative gifts is the ability to generate kidney stones at an alarming rate; just last year I had four in the left kidney. Between the time lost to pain and discomfort and more time lost getting diagnosed and treated, and then recovering from the treatment, between two and three months of that year were sacrificed to illness. When all the test results came in, the doctor gave me a list of things I must avoid. Of course, tea was one of them.

What made this really difficult was the close connection tea had to my writing. Could I still work without this wonderful part of my ritual? Yes, I could. Now I brew a pot of tea only once a week; it's become a little luxury. The rest of the time my writing ritual includes sucking down water a quart at a time; a half-gallon bottle is always with me. It's not a change I've particularly enjoyed, but it beats surgery any day.

It is possible to receive the creative life as a gift full of mystery and wonder and yet embark upon it with specific practices and consistent work.

✒ EXERCISES FOR A WRITER'S FORMATION

Mapping My Creative Process

These two things nearly always happen when I create:

During a creative work, I nearly always experience a particular emotion, _____, and this is when I usually experience it:

When I create something, this is what the beginning is like:

This is what the middle is like:

This is what the end is like:

My creative gifts really kick in when . . .

Other people get involved with my creative process in these ways:

During my creative process the low point for me emotionally is . . .

The high point for me emotionally is . . .

The Story of a Work

Tell the story of one of your creative works in two to three pages. It can be from any time in your life and any kind of creative work—perhaps a painting, a poem, a fancy dinner, a quilt.

Your story will include these points:

- an inciting incident—whatever gets the project started
- a goal or prize
- conflict—a hindrance that gets in the way of the goal
- an enemy or nemesis
- a friend or comrade
- the moment of greatest despair
- the moment of biggest decision
- climax
- resolution

Not all of these elements will be present in the factual story, but try to work in as many of them as possible.

Practices for the Creative, Spiritual Life
List practices in each category:

- practices for beginning work
- practices for centering/focusing
- practices that free me to explore and allow creative flow
- practices that include community
- practices for emotional health/equilibrium
- practices for filling up
- practices for the middle of a work
- practices for giving to others
- practices for finishing/letting go

There is something deep within us, in everybody, that gets buried and distorted and confused and corrupted by what happens to us. But it is there as a source of insight and healing and strength. I think it's where art comes from.

FREDERICK BUECHNER, IN *OF FICTION AND FAITH*

Find a character, like yourself, who will want something or not want something, with all his heart. Give him running orders. Shoot him off. Then follow as fast as you can go. The character, in his great love, or hate, will rush you through to the end of the story.

RAY BRADBURY, *ZEN IN THE ART OF WRITING*

I was gathering images all of my life, storing them away, and forgetting them. Somehow I had to send myself back, with words as catalysts, to open the memories out and see what they had to offer.

RAY BRADBURY, *ZEN IN THE ART OF WRITING*

There is ecstasy in paying attention. You can get into a kind of Wordsworthian openness to the world, where you see in everything the essence of holiness, a sign that God is implicit in all of creation.

ANNE LAMOTT, *BIRD BY BIRD*

For many writers and artists, the themes that predominate in their work also dominate their memories. To some degree, this is true for all of us. The past shapes our visions, which in turn define what we'll see and what we'll seek.

GREGG LEVOY, *CALLINGS*

4 THE VARIOUS WAYS
WE TAP THE WELL

*Where to Search for
Material and Inspiration*

About once a month I go to Amazon.com to look for any new customer reviews of my books. Usually people post a review only if they like the book, but there was one review of the first novel, *Grace at Bender Springs*, that came from an upset customer. This person decided that the book was much too sexual to be sold by a Christian publisher. The reviewer then listed the characters and their individual sexual preoccupations.

The fact is, there's not a phrase or sentence of explicit sex in the whole book. For the most part I think that explicit sex scenes, even if well written, are too jarring to enhance the forward motion of a story. An activity that in real life, is quite private and personal is difficult to translate in a way that is comfortable and natural for the reader. And I knew better than to attempt anything like that in a book that would be sold to a fairly conservative Christian audience.

The reviewer was picking up on the sexuality that I had refused to edit out of the characters' lives. I had chosen to be open to the unspoken fears and desires emerging from each character's sexuality, and this gave a lot of power to the story. It did not provide an atmosphere that would appeal to someone looking for a prurient thrill. But neither did it protect readers from a dynamic that's nearly always at work in human relationships. Bad reviews notwithstanding, I would not approach *Grace* any differently. Frankly, you cannot create an honest portrayal of a seventeen-year-old boy or a young widower or a wife and mother in her thirties and leave out the longings that can appear to be merely sexual but issue from much deeper desires.

When you give yourself to art, you must open wide the doors. If you are to see the whole character or the whole sky, all the light must be let in so that every angle and shadow can be studied. That doesn't mean that the final art will reveal every angle and shadow. But the artist can make better choices when there are more to choose from.

When you open up to life at its fullest, you may feel a little giddy. Actually, you may be filled with sheer terror. Learning to be open is not easy, for you or for some of the people around you. Openness subjects you to the unknown, and often the most religiously minded people have trouble with that. We turn to religious belief for many reasons, and a major reason is our desire for safety. Well, openness does not enhance a feeling of safety, which is why openness alone is not enough.

The inherent unsafeness of being open is the reason I placed this chapter *after* the previous chapter about submission to the creative process. When you are submitting, in faith, to that divine process and the God who oversees it, you can afford to be open.

﹏ TAPPING THE WELL

Much inspiration will come from your observations of the life that goes on all around you. But openness to life in general isn't usually what causes you to shiver and doubt. What takes real courage is openness to your own soul. Most of the scary stuff is right there.

Think of your soul as a great well. At the top and mouth of that well is your conscious life—your thoughts, opinions, known emotions and accessible memories. Down a little deeper is your unconscious life—

your dreams, intuitions, the memories you're not always conscious of. Deeper still—so deep that it flows from the groundwaters that connect you to other people—is what I call the Beyond Conscious. Some psychologists would call it the collective unconscious. Many Christians would call it the communion of saints. Whatever you call it, this deepest part of you is what connects you to the larger world of souls, the "great cloud of witnesses" mentioned in a New Testament letter.

Your well goes down deeper than you know, and it has been gathering information for a very long time. When you are doing work that is truly creative, you are tapping the well. You will tap a lot of things that are already in your life but that you just weren't aware of—such as your fears and desires, or the physical sensations of walking through a day. Sometimes you tap memories you didn't know you had or information you didn't realize you'd learned. From time to time you tap information you really haven't learned, at least not in a conscious way.

The more I talk with artists, the more convinced I am that mystical experiences are not uncommon in the course of creative work. (Here I use *mystical* in its most generic sense.) That's because sometimes creativity taps that deepest—beyond conscious—part of the well. My sense is that your soul knows when it's time for you to tap this or that, so bringing up material from these depths is not the same as *seeking* material. One of the beauties of creative work is that it is based in the spiritual life and can thus take you where you need to go when the time is right. Perhaps you need healing that has to do with family dynamics on your mother's side. As the story you're writing unfolds, you unwittingly hit upon some event that happened two generations ago in your mother's family. This sudden knowledge is a gift. Be grateful for the insight, and continue with your writing. Such inspiration cannot be forced. But neither should it frighten you.

Some people who tap the deep parts of the well claim to have paranormal gifts. I rather suspect that we all have the ability to tap those depths but our cultural and religious training has dulled the intuition by which we do this. In earlier centuries, mainstream religious communities (including the early Christian church) accepted dreams and visions as inherent to the spiritual journey. In the twenty-first century, in our overly rational Western culture, we are beginning to look again at the more intuitive and mysterious side of the human personality. The intuitive aspects of creativity can make it possible to tap the depths. When I mention this in a workshop, it's not uncommon for someone to come to me later in private and tell of having experienced some strange tapping of information that he or she had never had access to.

So I am more and more convinced that tapping the Beyond Conscious happens quite often in the process of creative work. I don't consider it occult or even scary, only fascinating—and not something to be sought, any more than I would seek mystical visions from Jesus. When we seek after the mystical in creative work, we're missing the point. The creative work may or may not tap deep memories or unknown wisdom, but whatever it taps must ultimately serve the work itself. Getting overly enthusiastic about mystical experience in the course of creativity is like worshiping angels rather than celebrating the rare occasions when we knowingly encounter them.

Much of what is in the depths of your well is family and regional history. What happened to your ancestors does have an impact on you. Christians are familiar with the Bible verse that refers to the sins of the fathers being visited upon subsequent generations. And in recent years there has been discussion of healing that is intergenerational, addressing damaging behaviors that have persisted down a family line until one person decides to seek healing and restoration. All of this has to do with our connection with the past. Even our physical location has meaning, something Native Americans and other tribal peoples have long recognized. All of this stuff is in your well, waiting to inform your creative work.

HOW WE TAP THE WELL

Here is a short list to get you started thinking about all the connections to the well that are available to you:

- memories
- dreams
- desires/fears
- senses
- beliefs
- emotions
- sexuality

You may be very comfortable working in some of these areas but not in others. You may have shut off some of them entirely, considering them not useful to you or even bad for you. Sooner or later you will need to get comfortable with these, and more, means of tapping rich resources.

✒ MEMORIES: LAYERS OVER LAYERS

Our memories are neither pure nor accurate. Their purpose goes far beyond recording history, whether personal or of larger scope. We remember events the way we need or want to remember them. Subconsciously we pick and choose the details; we attach feelings to those details. Our memories speak volumes about who we are, not because they recount what has happened to us but because they reveal what is important to us.

Memories are laid down in layers within us. The top layers are easy to access; middle layers will come up with some prompting; and some of them lie so deep that we don't reach them naturally and sometimes don't reach them at all. A memory is often connected to us in more than one way, and so the memory can be lifted into conscious light through some event or sensation when we aren't even looking for the memory. I once wrote a Bible study guide about angels, and it wasn't until my grandmother read that little book that she remembered an encounter she'd had as a very young woman when she was traveling alone and was helped by a gentleman who disappeared after she'd turned away for a moment. That had happened decades ago, and she'd had no reason to remember it. When she read my book about angels, the memory came back clearly.

Many of our memories don't surface easily or right away. Sometimes a present event triggers them. Sometimes a crisis of soul brings them out of hiding. They serve our soul development, but they are servants who live deep in the basement or way up in the attic, and much of the time we forget that they're even in the house.

As your spiritual life develops, your soul will bring up the memories that are attached to whatever work you need to be doing now. As your creative life develops, it—very creatively, I might add—rummages around in your memories for that perfect old hat or doll baby. Your creativity won't necessarily be looking for items that serve a higher purpose than to dress up the scene you're writing.

The reason creativity so enjoys memories is that they are loaded with emotion. Thus when we handle them in our art, we cannot help but become truly engaged, and the art that sings most magnificently is the art coming straight from our passion, from something with which we are fully engaged. You will come across memories when you are doing creative work because your creative self knows how well they work. You will come across them in your soul work because they hold keys to understanding yourself. And sometimes a memory will be truly efficient and give a hand to both the spiritual and creative aspects of your life.

If you don't have many memories, don't worry. Soul work and creative work will find them. You would be amazed at what a few little writing exercises can do for tapping memories. The more you hunt for them, the better you get at it. Memory is like a muscle that is flabby in most of us. As you exercise it, it will do amazing things.

You may possess some memories that are best left alone. These memories are too traumatic to handle, or for whatever reason you are unable to face them. But if they are so powerful that you are avoiding them, then they are probably manipulating you in subconscious ways. It seems that we generally remember things when something within senses that it is time to remember them. You don't need to go hunting for your deepest, darkest memories. But if you encounter them in the midst of your creative work, you may need some help with them through a counselor or spiritual director. If you are writing a poem, just going about your business, and something emerges that's ugly and makes you want to slam the door, chances are that your deeper, wiser self decided you could begin to deal with that ugly thing now.

When I was in the early stages of writing *Velma Still Cooks in Leeway,* I decided to spend some time in the book of Ezekiel. The issues I wanted to explore in the story were forgiveness and the need for healthy leadership in the faith community. Ezekiel includes wonderful passages about the "shepherds of Israel," in which God delivers scathing judgments on leaders who are not caring for the people. So I dwelt in Ezekiel for a month or so, just soaking up ideas and images.

One image that struck me was in chapter 3, verse 14: "The spirit lifted me up and bore me away; I went in bitterness in the heat of my spirit, the hand of the LORD being strong upon me."

These words gave me the idea for my book's title character, a middle-aged café owner named Velma. She was an ordinary person in a little Midwestern town, but I would give her "fever dreams"—times when she fell into fever and was carried away in dreams that said something about what was happening in her life. I would give Velma an experience suitable to an Old Testament prophet. So the very first sentence of the book reads, "When I was a young girl, strange fevers would fall upon me."

That was the progression: I chose the theme of the book, which led to reading Ezekiel, which led to giving Velma strange fevers.

About a year after the book came out, I was talking to my mother, and the discussion fell upon how sick I was as a kid—thyroid problems and medications that brought on other complications. At one point she mentioned "those fevers." I asked, "What fevers?" She reminded me of how I would get sudden high fevers as a child. I said I didn't remember that—was she sure it wasn't just fevers from the mea-

sles and other childhood maladies? She looked surprised: how could
I forget those awful fevers? She assured me that I would spike 104-degee
temperatures for no apparent reason, and all they could do was try to
bring them down with cool sponge baths.

Well, I had certainly forgotten them, yet they hadn't forgotten me.
Somehow the deep memory had connected with my thinking process
for Velma's story. Mom had assumed that I was writing from memory
when I put the fever part in the book. I still can't call up any memory
of sudden high fevers. That's okay; they emerged when my book was
ready for them.

Memories are powerful. Trust your interior self to find them when
the time is right. For now, remember that they are part of your life.
They help you become a whole person spiritually, and they give exuberant life to your artistic endeavors.

DREAMS: A REALM OF THEIR OWN

I've always been reluctant to work much with my dreams. You run
into some people whose life practically revolves around their dreams.
They keep copious dream journals, and no matter what your problem
is, their answer for you is to do "dream work." I've done some dream
work, but I've had to fit it in with a lot of other journaling and writing.

As we learn to pay attention to our dreams, an entire dimension
opens up. I give them more of my attention now. There are some
books designed to help you understand your dreams, such as the classic by Morton T. Kelsey, *God, Dreams and Revelation: A Christian Interpretation of Dreams.*

To put it in simple terms: Dreams are working on your interior stuff
while you are sleeping. They take your fears and anxieties, your joys
and discoveries, and they unpack them more than you are able to in
the course of a typical day. They work out problems, urge you toward
better relationships, tell you what you *really* think and what you *truly*
want. We are rarely in touch with those things, because we censor
ourselves all day long. A coworker may have hurt your feelings, but

you've got a deadline to meet, and it's very unprofessional to burst into tears and let out your feelings at the copy machine. So you push all that aside, deal with the traffic, throw together the evening meal, watch a stupid sitcom and go to bed. But when you finally get to sleep, your subconscious mind sifts through all the crap of your day and does damage control. It's quite a wonderful system.

If you decide to remember your dreams and think about them, your subconscious will often cooperate, and you will in fact remember what you've dreamed. It takes some direction to learn how to interpret dreams, because the dream world teems with symbols, and if you don't normally think symbolically, you will attach some very weird conclusions to your dreams. Dream experts warn us that we can rarely take a dream's meaning literally. So if you begin to pay attention to your dreams, get some practical assistance from a book or a person who has experience with dream interpretation.

After a while you will get acquainted with the particular symbols your subconscious likes to use. For instance, a huge orange truck has shown up in my dreams several times when I was about to take on a big endeavor. Flashy orange is hardly representative of my introverted self, and handling huge machinery is a frightening concept. In one dream my father thought I wasn't up to the task, but my husband encouraged me to get behind the wheel—thus I discovered that I had made a shift from relying on my father's perceptions of me to trusting more my husband's. I had been married a couple of years but was still clinging to the words and opinions of my father; this dream provided good news on that front. I recognize the big orange truck now and understand that it usually symbolizes positive movement for me.

It's important to remember that symbols mean different things to different people. A few of them are practically universal and will often mean the same thing across the board. But the only way to understand your dreams is to spend time with them.

The major spiritual traditions recognize the significance of dreams. The Bible's Old Testament recounts many stories involving people who both dream and interpret dreams. Recent scientific studies have indicated that dreams do in fact sometimes tell us things we wouldn't otherwise know. There are various theories about the purpose of dreams, but no one seems to argue their significance to the human personality. So if you choose to be more intentional about your dream life, you can pursue it with books or tapes, a spiritual director or a dream analyst.

What do dreams have to do with creativity? Have you ever turned a dream into a short story? Probably not. Dreams are not great raw material for artistic works because they are highly symbolic rather than sensual and specific. Some dreams may tell you precisely what you need to know; they do work out problems for you, and sometimes they may work out a problem you're having with a plot or a character. A number of great thinkers and inventors have worked out complicated solutions in their sleep.

But the main purpose dreams serve your creativity is the maintenance work they are doing in your interior life. They are tending the clutter that builds up day after day. And you're much more creative when you're uncluttered. This is why it is ultimately self-defeating for artists to go without sleep for long periods in order to finish some work. Most of us pull the occasional all-nighter. But if on a consistent basis you're not getting your dream sleep, your interior self is turning into a pigsty, and you are not at your best creative and spiritual self.

✎ DESIRES AND FEARS: OUR PERSONAL TRAPDOORS

Desires and fears come from deep within us. They can be tricky. Sometimes it's as if a trapdoor has suddenly opened beneath you, and you have fallen straight into the truth about yourself. Who knows where our desires and fears originate? I'm convinced that often they predate our actual life, that parents and grandparents set up patterns of fear and desire that get passed on to us in subtle ways. Wherever they come from, they are powerful, and for this reason we must get acquainted with them.

One of the negative tendencies of the religious tradition I grew up with is that it has consistently made people afraid of their own desires. I developed a deep-seated belief that if I wanted something a lot, it was probably bad for me. Whatever "God's will" was for me was something I was going to have to learn to like, such as boiled beets or tofu. In the general atmosphere of Midwest America, desires have always been suspect and assumed to be at odds with a holy, productive life. I have rarely heard it preached from a pulpit that our desires are in fact good—and may actually be God's desires.

This is one issue that sometimes separates creative people from certain religious communities. A creative temperament longs to drink deeply of life. To create is to explore all the tastes and textures and sounds of the universe. Natural desires are the perfect means for this exploration. But often the religious life is a structured life of rules and regulations. In such an environment, desires must be kept in check. I have had to learn to trust my desires much more than my upbringing allowed.

When we deny ourselves knowledge of our desires, we are withholding from ourselves some of life's richest materials. We are killing the senses that God created so that we might live life fully. I do believe in the reality of evil, but I do not equate evil with desire. I don't believe that our God-given desires lead us to evil. Many other things lead us there: fear, dishonesty, avoidance, a false sense of power. But our true desires will take us to what is truly good for us. This is what desires are designed to do.

What do you really desire—today, this year? Stop and ask yourself this question periodically. You may answer: *I want a real vacation.* And maybe that's what you want at one level. But that desire may be telling you that the deeper desire is for the ability to rest and refuel, vacation or no vacation. The first question may be, *What do I really want?* And the follow-up question could be, *Why do I want this?*

The key is to know what a true desire is. Does the married woman really want to flirt with that attractive man? Or is her true desire to feel that she is still attractive even after years of marriage, kids and a busy life? Does the young man desire to leave his home in the city? Or is this desire to flee covering the truer desire to be at peace in his workplace and to feel cared for in his circle of family and friends? We are constantly disguising our true desires because they are deep and they matter a lot, a whole lot, and we are scared to death that they are too tall an order.

I believe that the universe waits for us to follow desires that are too tall an order. When we desire big things, God is ready to step in with the grace and the growth. It's better that I long for peace in my marriage rather than cover that desire with the "need" to suddenly look twenty-five again. I'll go further in my soul development if I desire the best use of my creative gifts rather than concoct a desire to climb some social or financial ladder. My life will be healthier overall if I desire that novel that needs to be written rather than chase after the blockbuster that is sure to get picked up for movie rights.

I believe that my deepest, truest desires are actually the Creator's desires for me. As a Christian, I have been walking with Jesus for nearly thirty years now, and if the "right desires" haven't formed in me by now, I'll just not worry about it anymore. Unless you are actually motivated by hateful goals, your true desires are taking you along a continuum that leads to a wiser, truer you. Your deep desires are located in that well that is your very soul, and God created our souls to constantly move us toward health and wisdom and peace. Within your soul's mysteries is hidden the vision of what you are becoming. Trust your soul to help you get there.

As a creative person, you will burst into bloom when you create out of your desires. When you create from your passion, your words and images and sounds will become more than what they are. Your desires are buzzing with energy, with vivid detail, with visions that are beyond you. Give those desires their heads.

I've discovered lately that I have finally become what I played at being when I was a child. I was always making books and writing stories.

It took twenty years and a change of careers before I rediscovered that original desire and started writing in earnest. The lesson from this: spend time remembering what you loved as a child, before other people told you what was sensible. You may have to go back years to discover what it is you've really wanted. Unfortunately your family life may have clamped down on any desires you came close to forming, so that childhood memories are of little use to you now. Still, consider the days when you were absolutely in touch with dreams for yourself. Maybe you were five or maybe you were fourteen. Those early desires were probably very honest and uncluttered, and possibly they have something to tell you now.

Fears are the flipside of desires, and we need to know them for the same reasons. Fears are often connected to our desires, in that our greatest fears are that we will lose what we love and desire most. The worst thing about fears is that they slam doors all over the place. They slam doors between you and other people, and they slam doors inside you, in the interior self that has so many lovely places to explore.

Creativity might just take you straight to your fears. It might be a helpful exercise to pick a fear and explore it through your art. You never know—your creativity might be a safe place in which you can face your fear.

Over the past few years my creativity has taken me to explorations of the interior world. I've been more intentional about working with the subconscious, teasing things out of memory and desire. My creative work has given me a whole new sense of that spiritual realm into which all of us tap in various ways, whether through our gifts or our dreams or our prayers. Suddenly that spiritual realm is not so frightening anymore. And as a result I have been freed from fears that I had assumed would always bind me up. I give the credit to creative work.

Fears can have as much—or more—power than desires. You may be doing a lot to accommodate your fears. By dealing with fears through your creative work, you can bring them out of the subconscious and thus actually face them. Consider making one of your fears the fear of your main character or the focal point of your next sculpture or painting, and see what happens. One therapist actually suggested that by giving a particular fear of mine to a character I was writing, I could gain enough objectivity about it to get needed distance from it in my own life. Since creativity works on us at a deep, intuitive level, it makes sense that at times it can make end runs around other parts of ourselves that keep hanging us up.

Further, it so happens that when you infuse creative work with an emotion that is quite real to you, such as fear, the creative work takes on a dimension of reality that enables it to communicate powerfully to others. Your fear may as well serve a positive function for a change.

✎ SENSES: GIFTS OF AWAKENING

Allow me to describe my own weekly worship in terms of the five senses. There is Bach reverberating from the pipe organ or a southern hymn emanating from singers and mandolins; there are stained-glass windows and tapestries and candles; there is the heft of a hymnbook, the texture of another's hand when we pass to one another the peace of Christ; there is the taste of bread and wine; there is the smell of breezes wafting through in summer and radiators heating up in winter; there is the incense, the kneeler, the lights, the babies fussing. If nothing else, all of this forces me to wake up after a late Saturday night and see that God is still around and that people and things are the main vehicles in which I glimpse God passing by.

One surefire way to make writing dull is to make it abstract rather than concrete. Having worked in religious publishing for years, I've had my share of projects in which I had to help an author move from formulating ideas to stimulating the reader's senses. There are periods in every person's life of faith when God is an idea, a theology, a philosophy, a dogma. But God is rarely *known* during those periods. The divine becomes real in the waiting room, at the hospital bed, in the desperation of soul at three o'clock in the morning. The divine becomes known to us through simple acts of grace: a plate of food shared, a flower braving the storm just so you can gaze on it the morning you really need it, the song that crackles through on the radio and somehow heals a little rift in your heart. God does not transform us without touching us, and physical people sooner or later must meet God through the senses. The senses are what, in the end, make our theology make sense.

Without our senses, our creative work would simply not exist. Artists are pretty good at paying attention to their physical world. But most of us favor some senses over others. Look at your writing or whatever you do as creative work. What senses most inform that work? Some writers overwhelm you with visual description, but you can read through chapter upon chapter without being reminded of how things smell. Even if you think you are engaged with your senses, check yourself. What is missing from your work? What physical senses does it stimulate?

What senses do you actually engage with on a daily basis? Do you pay attention to textures as well as sounds, to odors as well as appearances? When was the last time you got really sweaty-dirty, or tried to pick out the distinct sounds of various types of machinery in your neighborhood, or ate slowly enough to enjoy the subtle flavor of every vegetable?

If you have lost touch with those wonderful senses—tasting, touching, seeing, smelling and hearing—please do something about that. You may have a disability that deprives you of one or more of these, but there is still some part of your physical self that is able to experience the life around you. Take some time to develop your senses. I promise that your philosophies, ideas and beliefs will mean more to you when you have done this. You are a physical being who waits to be set humming with celebration.

Senses allow you to enjoy life. Sometimes the best thing to do is leave the computer or palette and go eat ice cream. That simple pleasure can wake you up and thus help your creative work through its next step.

⚂ SEXUALITY: WHERE SENSES MEET THE SPIRIT

I've always been fascinated by the "very God and very man" existence that the Christian tradition ascribes to Jesus Christ. Here was a person who was certainly a human being yet who claimed to be fully divine at the same time.

Throughout history some people have been upset at the idea that Jesus the divine was also quite physical and human. Other people have been upset at the idea that a human being would claim to be the Son of God and thus divine.

Here's a thought: what if Jesus was merely introducing to us the concept that *we* are in fact divine and human at once? What if we are actually much more spiritual by nature than we have ever recognized—or utilized? And what if our physical nature is much more mysterious and transcendent than we have ever imagined?

What if the perfect life is one that honors the body and the soul equally, holding both in an exhilarating tension from which genius and sainthood emerge?

I'm no theologian, but my creative life has drawn me to this conclusion: we are at our best when we honor the physical life as well as the spiritual life. In fact they are both, mysteriously, the same life. We spend our entire tour of earth learning how these two sensibilities work together to form us as whole people.

What does this have to do with creativity? For one thing, if we accept that the physical and the spiritual are facets of the same existence, then we visionaries must come back to earth a bit. We must give better attention to the physical aspects of life that we would rather minimize and get out of our way. We must listen to our body better and ascribe more importance to our physical desires and inklings. We must deal in a more passionate way with aching muscles, hunger pangs and sexual chemistry.

If we give equal time to spirituality, those of us artists who prefer to engage in life senses first must step back and learn contemplation and worship. We need to give room to thought as well as feeling, to overarching themes as well as gritty details. We need to accept that what happens to our interior life is very important and must eventually inform what we do with our physical self.

There's a powerful connection between the physical gift of creation and the soul gift of creation. We create new human beings through sexual intercourse. A person's forming and then growing inside another person is a mysterious and miraculous process—little wonder that it starts out with an activity that is so captivating. No matter how many degrees we acquire or how much power we possess, there's something about sex that turns us into blobs of excitement, passion and foolhardiness. It seems to involve mere moving parts, but somehow it's bigger than the sum of those parts.

Sexuality is more than sexual activity; it's the heart of our sensual selves. Sensuality hooks us into every aspect of life. It's the business of artists to live in the senses, because if they don't, they miss the right color, chord progression, shape or turn of phrase. And sex happens to be in the middle of the senses. It incorporates sight, sound, taste, touch and smell to a heightened degree, bringing them together better than any other single activity.

If you're sensual enough to be creative, then I suspect that you are tuned in to the world sexually. People who are in touch with their sexuality often have the advantage when it comes to creative work. Being in touch with one's sexuality is not the same as being sexually active, and this is the distinction that so many well-meaning folks fail to make.

Sex is a teacher, just as emotion or intuition is a teacher. Your sexual self has a lot to say to you, but you have to listen and not panic. Through your sexuality you learn about trust and fear, about celebration and alienation. Through sexuality you learn to experience life through something besides your beliefs and ideas.

The more you understand yourself as a sexual person, the better equipped you will be to deal with the relationships and situations that touch on that sexual nature. The more able you will be to love yourself without inappropriate loads of shame and fear. It is your business as a creative person to learn who you are. Especially if you fashion the materials of the soul—through sounds, images, words or motions—you must understand and love the sexuality of being human.

Why were we designed with a mind that can work in the philosophical and the abstract—placed within this messy, excitable body that requires constant care and that is chemically, physiologically attracted to other bodies? In the same way that we're meant to live in emotional, intellectual and spiritual fellowship with other people, we're designed to dwell in physical fellowship with others. We must deal with every indelicate detail of an infant's body, or that infant will not survive. We often need the assistance of others—a hand to steady us, a hug when we're grieving or lonely, care for our physical needs when we're ill or injured. And our sexual nature draws us to physical communion that can become the heart of a life with others.

As you recognize how much sexuality permeates everything, you can have quite a full sex life, even if you are unable to have an active sexual relationship. You can use that energy and impulse to power up the work you're doing. The desire, excitement, longing and infatuation that fuel sexual desire can generate art that is alive with all of those things.

I went through years of not being sexually involved with anyone. It wasn't the life I wanted, but it was the life I had. While I was never very content as a single person and I suffered a lot from loneliness and rejection, I managed a fairly healthy existence. I attribute much of this health to how engaged I was creatively. Songs and stories were my outlets. Furthermore, they were means of engaging with God. There were long periods when I didn't feel particularly loved by God; still, I could carry on some communication through the art. And I did not allow myself to shut down sexually—that is, I preferred to wrestle with the desire and the frustration rather than deny that those feelings existed. When I did marry and learn how to be in sexual relationship, it was more or less like stepping into the next room. The same desires were engaged, but now they were dedicated in large part to my husband.

When your soul opens up in the course of your creativity, you are very likely to experience a sexual revolution. You thought you were doing a spiritual, creative work, and suddenly your body is talking to you in more ways than you can count. Or you thought you were a philosophical artist, painting icons or writing sonnets of a highly symbolic nature, and you find yourself wanting to make love to every person you meet.

What is happening here? Has your art somehow corrupted you? No, you are simply waking up. Your whole self is waking up. Of course sexual awakening involves some risks. But the first step in dealing with those risks is the basic acceptance—and celebration—of your sexual nature.

We need spiritual directors who are not afraid of sexuality. At this point I would not send a young artist to a pastor for help with this; I am not confident that the typical pastor is comfortable enough with sexuality to be of much help. Developing artists need the friendship of people who have embraced sexuality rather than spiritual police who will tell them it's not right to paint nude people or to explore sexual themes in their writing. I think spiritual helpers of the right kind are few and far between. Yet artists-in-process need people who can help them be safe in this spiritual and sexual realm.

I hate seeing a young writer or musician get sidetracked by sexual entanglements. The person may think at the time that this is doing wonders for the art. But because sex is closely linked to the spirit, it may actually delay creative development when it happens at the wrong time with the wrong person.

Whether you attend to your sexuality or not, it is well worth your time and energy to explore this area and come to a better understanding. And it is important to understand where the true boundaries are for you. Some people are more sensitive than others, and even within traditional religious definitions, the boundaries for one person may not match the boundaries of another. Because of the impact sexuality can have on your life and work, getting acquainted with it is an important aspect of your creative formation.

BELIEFS: WHERE POWER DWELLS

This is a tough one. Beliefs go deeper than you think, and they are so much a part of your life that sometimes it's hard to separate them from everything else. Yet it's important for you to come to terms with what you really believe. You may think you believe some things, but in your soul of souls you never have been convinced of them.

You may have spiritual aspirations for yourself that are totally impossible given what you truly believe. For instance, if you're struggling without success to pray as much as you think you should be praying, it may be because deep down you don't think prayer makes any difference. You may set out to write a book about love, but if you have never embraced love for yourself, your book will be a false document. It's necessary for you to unpack your beliefs—the conscious ones and the unconscious ones.

You most likely do not believe everything you were taught as a child. As you embark on this creative, spiritual life, now is the time to be honest with yourself. Have the courage to let go of dead beliefs. If you're like me, once you let go of beliefs you will be compelled to search more than ever for what is true. Giving up beliefs is not the same as giving up God or spirituality. A true belief holds on to you, not vice versa. And our questions—even the scary ones—lead us to more knowledge and more growth than do our certainties.

Your true beliefs will edit your creativity without your notice. Your concepts of the world will determine what material you even recognize as material for creative work. It's similar to learning another language that is not from the same family of languages as yours. If you grow up not hearing certain sounds, you won't hear them even when they're spoken to you. You have to train yourself to hear a new sound. Just so you have to train yourself to think differently, to entertain new beliefs or at least new angles to the beliefs you already have. Otherwise your creative work will remain confined to certain views of experience. In not believing that there is another doorway in the wall, you won't look for the doorway. You may walk right past it and not see it, because you never considered that it could be there.

Sooner or later you must face your true beliefs and your true doubts. Once you do that, your creative work will have more integrity and vitality. Until then you will be split in your soul, trying to be the spiritual person you are unable to be. And you will create works that perhaps are lovely but are not true expressions.

✒ EMOTIONS: A RANGE OF APPROPRIATE REACTIONS

Trying to live spiritually and creatively without emotions would be like trying to put on a gourmet meal without having a third of the ingredients. There's no real substitute for cinnamon, for instance, or for fresh tomatoes. And everyone can take bites and say how nice the meal is, but deep down in most of us there is a clear sense of what a real tomato *would* taste like. We learn to live without a lot of things that could make our life rich.

There are times when you honestly can't get the ingredient. Good cooks learn to go with the flow, but if I can't get the right thing for this sauce, I'll just make a completely different sauce rather than do a bad job on the sauce I'd hoped to make.

When it comes to emotions, there are times when you've got most of them but one or two are simply not present. Seasons of anxiety, pain and sleeplessness will rob you of certain emotions, and that's just the way it is. Joyful times can make you forget what hopelessness feels like. You can't expect to have a handle on the full range all the time. But when you *never* experience a particular emotion, there's cause to be concerned. Somewhere in your soul a door has been slammed shut and padlocked. Your spiritual life—and your creative life as well—will not be healthy as long as this door stays shut. We were designed to experience a range of emotions, because life confronts us with a range of situations.

It's possible, believe it or not, to put too much cinnamon in cinnamon rolls. Likewise, too much of one emotion can overwhelm a person. Yet many of us learn to deal with life through primarily one or two emotions. Either you're worried or you're relieved. You're either joyful or depressed. Some of us get addicted to a high-low sort of existence; we're always in the middle of some crisis—everything is just wonderful or we are on the brink of desolation. Some people think they are being spiritual only when they are joyful. Yet every spiritual hero we know much about went through dark emotions as well as bright ones.

In American culture, and specifically Christian culture, we have somehow turned any negative emotion into wrongdoing. Anger is wrong; sadness is wrong; grief, anxiety and fear are wrong. And because we attach a sort of sinfulness to these emotions, we just decide we won't have them. We won't give in to them. We will deny that they exist in us. Thus a whole lot of people are trying to live like Jesus but are denying much of what Jesus dealt with day in and day out. Because they refuse to acknowledge anger in themselves, they never deal with anger—they just push it deeper. Because they decide that they aren't afraid, they deny their soul the opportunity to face fear in a way that brings growth. Because they can't possibly be sad—"because I have so much to be thankful for"—they virtually numb themselves to much of what goes on around them.

I had finished, I believe, draft three of *Velma Still Cooks in Leeway,* but I knew that something was missing. The story was good and the plot worked, but I had neglected an ingredient I could not identify. After some thought, I realized that the title character, Velma, was helping people in her community learn forgiveness, yet Velma had not faced her own need of it. I had essentially left out Velma's dark side. Whom did she need to forgive? Did I dare uncover her anger or bitterness? The story was already written, and I dreaded the thought of reworking the whole thing to include this lost aspect. But then I saw that I had already planted the problem in the back story; all I had to do was bring it forward.

This missing ingredient transformed the novel and rewrote the ending. And the power that it generated was much greater than what the story had possessed before. I'd been too easy on Velma because I liked her so much. But she had her sins too. She had that one thing that she clung to, that one wound for which she needed healing.

I urge you to allow the full range of emotions. You can't work with them until you let them in the room with you. Working with an emotion is not the same thing as indulging an emotion. Which brings us to the impact emotion has on creativity.

Creative people, by nature, immerse themselves in life experience. We love emotions because they are so colorful and so interesting. We wallow in emotions. We want to get every angle, every texture out of that emotion. And so we have symphonies that, without any words of interpretation, can make audiences weep. We have actors who with a single look can teach us powerful lessons about our own life. Emotions, when tapped, bring a dimension to a scene or a song that will make all the difference.

Sometimes we pay a price for the emotions we work with when we are creating. It can be difficult to delve into an emotional scene while I am writing a chapter of a novel but then to pull out of it by dinnertime. An artist sometimes has to live with certain emotions long enough to understand what they mean to a creative work. This can be exhausting. It can make it hard to communicate with those around you.

I've found it helpful to process my feelings while I'm working with emotional material. When I'm alone, I process by crying or laughing as I work. My novels contain a lot of tears.

A creative writing instructor once asked a student, after she had read her story, "Did you cry while you wrote that?" The student answered no, and the teacher replied, "Go back and write it again, only this time, cry." The student had not connected with the story enough to be moved, and so the writing didn't connect with any of us. She rewrote it, allowing the emotions to flood in, and we could certainly tell the difference when she read the revision to us.

I don't talk a lot about my writing while I'm writing, but sometimes

I do talk through the emotional part of it. It's a release when I can read a passage to my husband. If it's a passage that came through with a lot of emotion that stirred me up, I'll read it to Jim; he can react to it, and we talk about it, and that helps me get past that emotion. I don't have to be overwhelmed for hours and days on end.

Any artist will have to find ways to process emotional work. Sometimes there is no easy way, and you will have to bear with those difficult emotions as long as you're doing a particularly tough project. Explain this as best you can to the people you live with. Spouses, kids and colleagues may need to give you some space, some room for a little craziness. On the other hand, you must look for ways to give your soul some breathing room. Perhaps a habit of prayer will help. Or maybe physical exercise will provide a pressure valve. You are doing spiritual work, and the emotion is part of what makes it powerful. But you are also living your own life in the midst of it, and you owe it to yourself and those around you to take care of yourself. Find what works for you.

Inspiration All Around

While much of our inspiration and material grow out of our own experiences, there is much to be found in the exterior life. As you develop your powers of observation, the ideas will multiply. Here are a few ways to practice openness to the world around you.

Pay Attention to the News

I confess that I don't read newspapers very often. I don't feel that it is my moral duty to follow daily headlines or to stay updated on the lives of celebrities. I tend toward magazines, including some alternative press sources. But I know that if I ever need more material for writing, one trip through some newsprint will inspire something.

To get the best creative use from a newspaper, skip the front-page stuff. Go to the lesser headlines. Take the headlines or first paragraphs of two unrelated stories and put them together. Take one interesting situation and free associate for ten minutes by writing, painting or dancing whatever comes to mind.

Be sure to read alternative newspapers and magazines; they cover the stories that the more mainstream companies don't consider marketable enough. All the major newspapers and magazines are controlled by a handful of corporations, and their financial interests sometimes prevent balanced coverage. They are also less likely to pick up on the odd little story that could birth an entire creative work for you.

Pay attention to the events right around you, whether or not they merit media coverage. What's happening in your neighborhood, your apartment complex? Watch and listen on buses and trains, in restaurants (including glimpses into the kitchen) and at community events.

Get Acquainted with History

I firmly believe in the communion of saints. Through my present life I can interact with the lives of those who have gone before, and their lives can inform what I do now. That communion can happen in intuitive, unexplainable ways. But often it happens through a simple examination of history.

By looking back on a situation, we can open up a topic or a person in a way that was impossible during that person's lifetime. A situation from centuries ago can provide a different angle from which to view a current dilemma. There are lessons to learn from the past that cannot be revealed until the past is reopened creatively during this era by a specific person exercising her specific creative gift.

Explore the past through your own ability to observe, analyze and visualize. Choose a war, a subculture, a major event or a minor character, and open it up for a new look. Vincent Van Gogh revealed a mining community in his early paintings; the film *Gosford Park* gave an interesting view of social classes in England; the film *Babette's Feast* provided an amazing glimpse, through a feast, of giftedness.

Absorb the Creative Work of Others

There is a long list of films that evolved because a writer or filmmaker studied another creative—an artist such as Picasso, an idiot-savant pianist or a B-film director such as Ed Wood. These somewhat biographical works are important and inspiring in and of themselves. But sometimes the creative work of another person will birth the idea for another work of art completely—and apart from the persona of the original artist.

I once wrote a monologue from the viewpoint of a fictitious boy who observed the crucifixion of Christ. It had to do with throwing stones at Roman soldiers—a rather intentional reference to the stone-throwing Palestinian children in the Occupied Territories. One line of the monologue was about how the stones seemed to sing as they flew through the air. I read the monologue during a church service. A poet in the congregation subsequently wrote a poem about singing stones. He would not have thought about that subject if I had not first introduced it in another medium. There are songwriters who write about the works of artists, novelists who explore the worlds that birthed musical genius, filmmakers who invent stories around the mathematical or scientific innovations that changed an era. These are powerful creative expressions that not only illuminate the gifts of others but also allow us to view the world through multiple lenses.

You will never run out of ideas for your creative work, if you pay the least attention to your inner world as well as the one that surrounds you. Openness is a gift, but it is also a skill that gets better with practice.

◈ Exercises for a Writer's Formation

Your Well
Draw a picture of your well. At the top is your *conscious life*. The next level down is the *unconscious life*, which includes your dream life, your fears and desires, and your memories. The third level I call the *Beyond Conscious life*, which includes your family history, the "communion of saints," the "collective unconscious" or whatever else you want to call it. Describe or draw items that you feel are prominent in each of these levels of your well.

Life Through the Senses
Everything in this day was in vivid color. I'm going to walk through the memory of this day slowly now and describe all the colors, what they did, how they felt, what they meant to me.

Everything in this day made some sort of noise. I'm going to walk through the memory of this day slowly now and describe all the sounds, what they did, how they felt, what they meant to me.

Every part of my day was full of textures. I'm going to walk through the memory of this day slowly now and describe all the textures, what they did, how they felt, what they meant to me.

I experienced today primarily by how it tasted. Here are all the flavors, where they happened and how they affected me.

When I walked through today, all I saw were shapes. This is how it was:

The Emotional Landscape

The last time my own anger frightened me was . . .

I've had the most satisfied feeling about my life when . . .

I didn't understand what real joy was until . . .

The happiest surprise I ever had was . . .

The worst shock I ever received was . . .

I didn't know true sorrow until . . .

I try to be open-minded, but I get really disgusted when . . .

Beliefs and the Senses
Come up with a phrase or statement that describes a belief you have about life.

Expound on this phrase or statement. Your finished piece needs to include the following:

- a taste
- a texture
- a fragrance
- an image
- a sound
- a dream
- a desire
- a memory
- a positive emotion
- a negative emotion

When you take the responsibility for performing for an audience, you are then accepting the fact that you must go through some sort of distilling process in which the personal experience has become so zeroed and so heightened by a clarity that you know exactly what you're dealing with, in terms of the element. You have so much skill that you can get right down to the essence of that element.

ANN HALPRIN, IN CREATORS ON CREATING

It is true that the logical left deserves the credit for grammar, punctuation, format—all essential to writing anything readable. But the right hemisphere has style. It has rhythm. It has the flow and the energy of excitement when you're on a roll. It provides images and analogies, color and music—in short, everything that lifts your written piece . . . from the mundane and predictable to the inspired and inspiring, the unforgettable.

HENRIETTE ANNE KLAUSER,
WRITING ON BOTH SIDES OF THE BRAIN

Good-heartedness and sincerity are no substitute for rigorous pursuit of the fictional process.

JOHN GARDNER, THE ART OF FICTION

Sometimes the writer leaves his early chapters in place from gratitude; he cannot contemplate them or read them without feeling again the blessed relief that exalted him when the words first appeared—relief that he was writing anything at all. That beginning served to get him where he was going, after all; surely the reader needs it, too, as groundwork. But no.

ANNIE DILLARD, THE WRITING LIFE

5 THE BALANCE THAT
LEADS TO GREATNESS

How to Craft but Not Control
While Using Both Sides
of the Brain

I despise anything numerical. This serious avoidance is most likely rooted in eighth-grade math class, which was my first occasion of academic struggle. The frustrating part was that I could understand mathematical concepts pretty quickly; it was the adding, subtracting, multiplying and dividing that messed me up. I was forever making stupid errors. And if the answer is wrong, it doesn't matter that you understand the formula. All I remember about that year of math is being on the verge of tears regularly and feeling stupid most of the time. I also remember that although several other girls chewed gum in math class all the time and never got caught, the first time I tried it I got caught and was reprimanded. Ah, the trivial things that cause damage to a forming self-image.

In college I plunged happily into life as a music major, but certain aspects of music are expressed numerically, and music theory is composed of formulas—certainly not complicated ones, but complicated enough for a person who is formula- and number-phobic. Although I had been writing music pretty well on my own, I stumbled and fretted through simple theory assignments. Then there was college algebra, the one class I actually feared flunking out of. I almost blew the final exam purposefully so that I could retake the course and not have the lowest grade on my record. The only reason I came out of Civil War history with a decent grade was that I wrote better essays and book reports than most of the grad students (the professor called me to his office to tell me this and inform me that as a sophomore I wasn't supposed to be taking this upper-level course but he'd let me stay anyway). I did not fare nearly so well on the tests, because they required a functioning memory of dates—not an unusual requirement in a history course.

So is it any wonder that I procrastinate when it comes to working out the timeline of a plot? Timelines involve dates and finite periods of days and weeks, and dates are numerical. And anything numerical I am very likely to miscompute.

But I fear embarrassing errors in the story line more than I fear the day or two of working and reworking numbers. So by draft two of a story I tackle the timeline, spreading out large sheets of paper and, to make it more interesting, using markers of various colors. I've discovered, though, that the timeline itself nearly always reveals a wrinkle of the story I'd never even considered. This numerical, very left-brained task possesses its own magic.

As an editor of more than a decade, I am confident that every manuscript has at least one glaring technical error in it. I become the technician for the writers I edit, bent on saving them from unnecessary embarrassment when the reviews come out. And I pray that my editor will save me from my errors. Sooner or later, one of us must get out a calculator or a calendar and make sure the numbers come out.

Imagine now a particular genius-artist. This woman must have at least two original visions per day. It's exciting just being around her. Her energy is catching. When she finishes a work, you know that she has definitely tapped into the greater Work.

When she finishes a work. That's a big *when*. As gifted as she is, she has a history of disrupted works and a capricious process. While she envisions works that are revolutionary, her creative drive sometimes appears to be a drive and nothing else: tremendous energy bouncing every which way and practically battering her senseless. Understandably, she suffers from great emotional highs and lows. She is forever launching into some new vision and then breaking down before it's finished.

Imagine also a writer of great promise and conviction. This man has enough wisdom to really transform the lives of his readers. You know this from spending time with him. He has churned out about ten books now. But each book is sort of a disappointment. You don't find in his written words the essence that made you want to read him in the first place. His arguments make perfect sense, and his logic is flawless. But the sentences themselves lack that luster, that life that words need if they are to wake up people and give them hope.

These are two hypothetical examples of creative lives that have not found their balance. In the first, you have an artist who is a great believer in the Muse. But she has not developed her craft well enough to deliver her vision. Neither has she developed enough analytical thinking to judge and shape her own work. Thus she is at the mercy of creative flashes, and she grows quickly frustrated when the flashes stop and she is left not quite knowing what to do.

In the second example, you have a man who, being a great thinker and motivated by holy convictions, is overconcerned about being in control of his work and that it make perfect sense. He has certainly experienced creative flashes, but he clamps down on them almost immediately by applying his analytical skills rather than giving creativity its head. To control the process, he maps out exactly what the book will be and does not deviate from it, rendering his creative intuition impotent and, eventually, silent.

As a book editor, I have known versions of both these people. It's so frustrating to see gifted artists burn out from creative energy that doesn't find the necessary structure or skill. It's equally frustrating to see gifted artists grow dull because they need to be in control and are afraid to allow the creative, intuitive self to speak freely.

It doesn't have to be this way. No matter what your natural inclinations are, you can learn to master your craft. You can also learn to allow the creative flow that gives you material to master.

A simple yet effective way to think about it is this: you must work with both sides of the brain. This analogy has been used for some time in the arts; more than a decade ago I read Henriette Anne Klauser's book *Writing on Both Sides of the Brain*. The right side of the brain is the creative, emotive, affective and intuitive side. When the creativity is flowing, when loads of interesting things are coming to mind, when you can hardly keep up with yourself because the ideas are coming so quickly, the right side of your brain is working. This "flow" is often mistaken for the work itself, but in reality it is only the beginning of— the raw material for—the work. When you allow a scene to float up into your head and you write it down without thinking much, your right side is operating.

The left side of the brain is the organized, analytical, logical, editorial side. When you step back from that creative flow and analyze what's happening, the left side of your brain is working. When you analyze the scene that spilled out during the right-brained creative flow, to figure out why it should be in the book and how to shape it accordingly, your left side is operating. Your editorial brain is what looks for gaps and flaws, what checks the grammar and makes sure the modifiers are in the right place.

Neuroscientists are discovering that the human brain cannot actually be divided up so simply. For decades we pictured it as an organ with compartments—this one for speech, that one for motor movement and so on. But it now appears that life in the brain is not so clearcut. So this right side/left side discussion is not technically accurate. But we can use these as symbolic terms for now, just to help us visualize the different functions that take place during the formation of a creative work. When I speak of left brain, I'll be referring to your inner editor and bean counter. When I speak of right brain, I'll be referring to your visionary and intuitive.

The point is, you need both sides of the brain to function if your creative work is to take full form. You need the intuition and vision, the emotion and image making, in order to have any material at all. You need the analysis, the logic and the editing in order to give the material shape and polish.

So to be effective in your creative work, it's necessary to learn how the analytical and intuitive work together. You need the skill required for good analysis and editing, and you must learn to trust the intuitive flow.

Remember that in the previous chapter on balance I referred to your soul as a deep well. This well is situated firmly in your life and in the life of your family, in the region and culture that shaped your family and in the history that produced you. When you are allowing the right brain to work, you are hauling material up out of this well. You are pulling images, memories, emotions, beliefs and so forth up out of the mysterious dark that is your subconscious and also the Beyond Conscious.

Drawing material out of this well is what your visionary, intuitive right brain does—and this function is something that your left-brained inner editor knows little about. Likewise, the right-brained intuitive self doesn't know what to do once the bucket's contents are spilled out. It is the inner editor, the left-brained self, that sorts out the contents, choosing the bits and pieces that will serve this particular poem or painting and tossing less useful items back into the well. It's sort of like having two people inside you, one pulling the material up out of the well and the other working with the material. One person is primarily generative, and the other is primarily analytical. They must work together.

We know that the process is not so simple and easily categorized, but a lot of creative folks find it helpful to think in these broad terms of two functions within the larger process of creation.

✎ THE PROCESS THAT CANNOT BE CONTROLLED

The truly creative process is not something you control. When you try to control it, you short-circuit the creativity. One reason I consider creativity to be highly spiritual is that it requires faith in the way that spirituality requires faith. In both realms you must believe that there is something bigger than you overseeing your life and keeping you safe. My Christian belief is that God oversees and protects my faith and my creativity. More and more they are one and the same to me.

Without this faith, it is easy to fear the creative process. This process is rooted in your spiritual, intuitive self, and there will always be much more that you don't know about it than what you do know. You will always possess, in a conscious way, just a small bit of the true picture; more of the picture unfolds as you allow creativity to flow. And in order to allow creativity to flow, you have to shut off your censors, your rules, your judgment—your editorial self. You have to allow the arrival of whatever comes. When you do, the creative process draws all sorts of material out of your well. Some of it will surprise you, some will disgust or even frighten you. But it's all material for you to work with, even if all that the work involves is your decision to throw something back.

Think of it this way. Not only is your soul bigger and wiser than you are, it knows the story better than you do too. You may begin a poem and think you know where it's going, but you're going on your conscious, limited knowledge. Your well contains the true end of the poem, and you simply won't know it until your creativity draws it up. All you can do is watch what appears at the rim of the well. During the generative flow, this is what you do. You begin writing or painting or whatever, and you just do what comes to you, and you watch what appears.

I write the early draft of anything without looking back. I don't worry about how any scene works or even if it will end up in the final book. I know that I'll have to go back and research some aspect of the story, but that will happen later. I don't think about whether this word works better than that word. I just type and watch what appears. As it all takes shape in front of my eyes, I know that much of it will change, but my job for the moment is to draw the material out of the well. That's all. That's the creative flow. I'm learning not to hinder it.

A creative process will keep secrets from you; all you can do is keep working until you discover the secrets. The process will feel good one day and terrible the next; all you can do is go with the mood and not analyze it. And the process will decide in the middle to make some major change, forcing you to rework the whole piece; all you can do is apply your skill to making the change.

We learn about ourselves as we come to trust the process. Since I've acquired more faith in my creativity, I've also acquired more faith in general. Now that I'm learning that the story will sooner or later find its proper ending, I'm coming to trust that my own life story will find its proper ending too. Creativity is thus a great spiritual instructor. Its slow unfolding teaches us patience and faith. We learn to adjust as the information changes—an extremely important lesson to apply to all of life.

If you find that you must outline everything and stick to that outline as though it were the Ten Commandments, you can be pretty sure that your generative flow is hindered. You're throwing things out of the bucket before it even reaches the top of the well.

When you choose to participate in creativity by trusting the process and allowing the flow to do what it will, you are making a crucial step as a creator and as a person. It's very healthy to accept that you're not in control of most things. You're not in control of other family members, of the weather, of that project at work, of the way a community program plays out. You're not in control, and you were never meant to be. You were meant to be a participant, that's all.

◁◈ THE CRAFT THAT MUST BE MASTERED

The reason you have no need to control the creative process is that you are becoming a master at your craft.

I had to go back and rewrite my entire first novel so that one of the major viewpoints changed from male to female. I traded the pastor's version of the story for his wife's version of it. This huge shift was possibly the best thing I could have done for the story.

This was no small task—changing an entire viewpoint. It required that I open up another character in the story, one who until then had been fairly minor. To close up the husband and open up the wife required skill as a writer. I had to rethink every part of that couple's story and transform it to how the wife would see it.

If I had not been able to rethink a story line and shift viewpoint, I could not have followed the creative flow of the book. In this case my editor saw what I couldn't; it was his creativity that recognized the mistake of viewpoints. But a published book is a collaborative process, and I trusted that the editor's opinion was an intrinsic part of the process. So I followed his advice and made the change. I could do it because my writing skill was up to it.

I've had to switch gears on the current novel, which I wrote for three years in the past tense. I realized during year four of the writing that it would probably work better in present tense. My skill had to be up to changing the whole book to a different tense. This is what a writer has to do; otherwise her career will be a short one.

It is perfectly all right to go with a book's process—to change plot points, rearrange events, kill off characters and introduce new ones—as long as you have the skill to make those shifts. Do you have a practiced ability to stop thinking one way and start thinking another way? Do you have the technical expertise to change the order of scenes in order to build the tension? Do you have what it takes to survive a totally different ending from the one you first envisioned? You can do all of this if you are practicing your craft.

You are not in control of the process by which your art is made. But you are the only one who can practice your skills so that you have the flexibility to track with the process. This is your job—to master your craft. For me it's learning how to make sentences work, how to shape scenes, how to flesh out characters. That's my work. That's what I practice. This skill is my contribution to the creative work. If you are mastering your craft, then you won't need to panic when all manner of strange stuff comes up out of your well. You know that as time goes by your skill will take hold of all that stuff and make something out of it. You know that as you develop your abilities you will know what to use and what not to use. And if a different ending pops up over the rim of the well, you know that your skills will take that ending and work with it and the rest of the story until they're a good fit.

One of my creative outlets is cooking. I cook from recipes, and I make up recipes. Over the years I've done enough cooking that I can substitute ingredients and make any adjustments necessary to bring most dishes to a satisfying conclusion. I tend to be more comfortable playing with bread recipes than with candy recipes, because I'm more experienced at making bread. I'm better with vegetables than with meats. I can wing it with casseroles and omelets and soups but not so much with fancy desserts.

My experience as a cook has raised my confidence to handle a variety of situations in the kitchen. If I'm out of one herb or spice, I figure out an alternative. And if something doesn't turn out as wonderful as I'd hoped, unless it's the main course for company I don't get upset, because there's always another dish and another meal.

My goal is to have a comparable comfort level with words, sentences, ideas and chapters. The longer I work with characters and plots, the more confident I am about solving problems and adjusting to whatever the creative flow brings my way.

How do you master your craft? By practicing the craft. By taking classes, reading books, observing other master craftspeople. Think of it as a job that you go to; you give it your best, put in your hours. On many days no magic happens, but you still do pretty good work. On the bad days, the best you can say is that it was a day of practice. And on the really good days you have something wonderful to show for your efforts.

❧ THE INTUITION THAT PROVIDES THE MATERIAL

The creative person inside you—the right side of the brain—needs a lot of space and understanding. He's sort of like the classic extravert who learns what he thinks by talking out loud. He spills information before it even makes sense. And he's so expressive while doing so—just full of passion, emotion and energy. Forget about getting him to break down his thoughts and put them in order—he can't do it. That's why he needs his partner, the introverted editor, the quiet self that stands by and studies everything that's flying out of Mr. Personality's mouth.

You have to just let Mr. Personality have his say. You have to be quiet and let him ramble. The moment you get critical or start asking questions, his feelings will get hurt or he'll become irritated and shut up. So just stand by and listen and watch. Take notes but be quiet.

When you allow the creative flow to happen without interruption, what comes up from the well could be almost anything. It may be fraught with emotion—or not. It may be connected to your dream life. It may bring up forgotten memories or add details to memories you already have. It often works by stream of consciousness and free association. This is work you do rather mindlessly—that is, you witness what's happening but you don't try to think about it. For some reason the stream of consciousness cannot flow when the more logical thinking process kicks in.

This is why so many inexperienced writers get writer's block. They try to edit before the generative flow is finished. They start thinking analytically too early, and so the material stops coming. This probably happens regularly to students who are trying to write to deadlines. Especially if you put off writing a paper until a couple of days before it's due, you've got no time to allow the creative flow to generate its material. And creative flow is important no matter what kind of paper you're writing. Intuition and vision work just as well for research papers as they do for short stories. You need to tap your deeper wisdom regardless of the topic or purpose of what you're writing. Yet most of our education about writing has to do with outlines, propositions and so forth. I'd like to see what would happen if teachers began incorporating "free writing"—the quick writing that you do automatically—into homework schedules. What would happen if students were encouraged and trained to tap their creative flow? If they had really interesting material to work with, then the left-brained part of it wouldn't be such a chore.

I can't stress enough that you can trust this flow. You can trust it because it is merely raw material; it is not the finished product that you're stuck with. Once you consider all your words raw material, you will be much freer to just write whatever comes. And you will also be much freer to do whatever you need to do with what comes.

You can't put this flow on a schedule. Sometimes the good stuff comes out of the well quickly; other times you haul up many decent ideas before you come to the one idea that works. If you're too hyper about getting that good idea right now, then you will likely rush the process and try to force something before its time.

One friend of mine heard an interview with a well-known comedian who had worked for years with a comedy troupe. He commented that a lot of the ideas that turned into the best comedy were not the first ideas that came up, so he had learned to be patient and allow a lot of ideas to generate rather than jumping at the early ones.

It's awesome when a really good sentence, or a powerful scene, or witty dialogue, floats across your brain. Sometimes the material arrives practically intact, and you feel that you've been given a gift. It seems inspired, coming from somewhere outside you. Many times I've written a paragraph, then gone back to read it and wondered how in the world I ever came up with it. It's like magic. Only it's not magic, and I need not worship it or preserve every word and phrase as though it were sacred.

The fact is, wonderful words and phrases will keep coming as long as I'm free to let them come. It's not magic; it's an intrinsic part of the human personality. It's the visionary intuition that Western culture has practically obliterated from its consciousness. Some days I still sit down and wonder if anything will happen when I place my hands on the keyboard. Sometimes I still feel that this word work of mine falls down from heaven. But it's not falling down from heaven. It's welling up from inside. God has already placed all that fascinating stuff in my life. It's mine to discover and work with.

A lot of fear regarding your creative life will subside when you accept that the most wonderful stuff is in you already. It's there and waiting to be found. It may get triggered by outside people and events. It may become clearer as you study the information in your environment. In fact, the more you are connected to the world around you, the better sense the stuff inside you will make. It was all meant to be synthesized. But you don't depend on outside sources for your creative genius.

What am I doing during this creative flow, this right-brained part of the process? Well, I can tell you what I do in the course of writing a novel. I take each character and free-write about him or her. I write whatever comes to mind, creating a history, a family, a personality. I try to pull up out of the well the whole character, even parts that won't appear anywhere in the book. In the fiction craft this is called the back story.

This is the only time I allow my characters to stand around and make long speeches. When I'm free-writing them, I'll let them go on for pages. I'll listen to them vent. I need to know what's going on inside them. I need to get acquainted with those deeply rooted emotions and hang-ups. Of course those long speeches won't make the final cut—because nothing kills the movement of a scene faster than a long speech. But during the right-brain phase of writing I let out all the stops.

In *Art in the Zen of Writing*, Ray Bradbury says that all you really need for a story is a character who has a passionate desire. The character and the desire will generate the plot. So one of the first things I do is figure out what each character's driving desire is, and I'll free-write on that.

I also free-write about the location of the story. I'll imagine what the Iowa countryside looks, feels and smells like in a given season. Or I'll create the interior of an old urban cathedral. It doesn't matter if I've never actually been to the place I'm describing. It's important that I generate the vision, which of course I'll check out later. Sometimes I'm able to go on location before I'm at the free-writing stage, but because this free-writing falls so early in the process, I am often writing in total ignorance. That's all right—it's good exercise. And it's surprising how many times my soul has had a pretty accurate reading even before I did the research.

The most fun part for me in this right-brained, free-writing phase is writing scenes. I write them in whatever order they come, when I feel like writing them. I put two characters in a situation and just let it unfold. I allow the argument to carry on for pages, or I allow a character's thoughts to spend far too long describing how the room feels and looks. Even as I'm writing, I know that I'll cut out most of the description and edit the argument, if I even keep the argument. But I write what comes. And sometimes that first draft of a scene holds its true essence, the key phrase or paragraph or turning point, and that's what I keep and use to shape the edited scene.

Sometimes I'll take a theme in the story and write about it. This helps me understand my own feelings and opinions about the subject of my story. Much of what you discover as you free-write, as you allow the creative flow to deliver its goods, is what *you* actually think and feel. Whether or not a book is autobiographical in obvious ways, you will always be present somehow in it. And sometimes you can't write the story well until you understand how you yourself really interact with its theme. Free-writing is great for this.

I need to mention at this point that being in the creative flow doesn't mean that you're not making any choices or doing any editing. Because I edit for a living, I edit by habit even when I'm free-writing. *But it's not editing that stops the process.* I'm merely making choices as I go. You will use analytical skills to some degree whenever you're working; you can't do creative work without making some choices. But when you shift

mental gears in order to stop and analyze, reread and edit, you have
likely stopped the creative flow. Such an overall shift should be avoided
until the creative flow has come to its own stopping point.

THE ANALYSIS THAT SHAPES THE MATERIAL

When I'm ready to shift from creative flow to a very conscious crafting
of the material, I usually need some time to get ready. It's a big shift,
and it harbors its own anxiety. Maybe when the creativity was flowing
I worried that the flow would somehow choke up. Now my fear is that
my skill isn't up to the job of sorting out what the flow has given me.

During this crafting process I will have to make thousands and
thousands of decisions. I will have to throw out material. I may have
to kill off a character or two. I'll probably have to rewrite extensively
in order to get the tense or the voice right. What I'm about to dive into
is a lot of hard work. It's satisfying, because I'm gifted to do it, and we
are generally deeply satisfied when we are doing what we're gifted to
do. But I know that I am embarking on a long, slow task.

Being out of the generative, right-side-of-the-brain mode doesn't
mean that my editorial crafting work is not creative. Even in the word
choices I make, my creative gifts are at work. But the process itself has
shifted. I am applying my analytical skills, something I don't allow
when I'm hauling material out of the well.

What do I work with when I'm in this left-brain stage? Well, as a
storyteller, I sketch out a plot as best I can. I've usually free-written
about characters, giving myself at least a page or two of information
about every person in the story. Now I take that information, set the
characters side by side and begin to analyze how these characters,
with their unique backgrounds and personalities, will interact with
one another. To look at all this I need to be logical. I need to ask myself
how a woman in her thirties whose career is in the navy will respond
to, say, a fifty-something Vietnam vet—or a fifty-something draft
dodger. What would the conversation be like between a sixty-year-old
Iowa farmer and a forty-year-old psychotherapist? I'm taking the raw

information about characters and putting it in some kind of order that tells me what these various relationships might look like. I'm also trying to figure out what viewpoint and tense will give the story its best voice. This is mainly by trial and error, but it's quite analytical. It's also creative—all of it is creative, but it's not the same as that initial creative flow. This work involves a more directed and thoughtful sort of creativity.

While in the left-brained mode, I work on timelines, I research the region where the story is set, I read what others have written about topics that appear in my plot. That's the big-picture work. At a later stage, when I'm rewriting scenes and chapters, I'm deciding, word for word, what works best. I'm rearranging sentences so that their order flows better for the reader. I'm asking myself, *Would a thirteen-year-old girl use that expression?* I'm tearing apart everything, pretending to be the most critical of all readers. At a very late stage I am reading every sentence, paragraph, scene and chapter out loud, so that I can catch the sorts of glitches that the eye might miss but the ear will recognize.

Analytical work carries its own fascination. I can get caught up in the flow of editing just as much as I get caught up in the creative flow that provided the raw material. These are two amazing parts of the same process. Both are engaging, both require energy, and both require their own form of faith and commitment.

One practical matter to remember: even as you hack away all the extra material, even as you edit ruthlessly, there's no law against saving everything. Most of the time I have an "extra" file in which I dump everything that I edit out. In some cases I just love the way I wrote a certain paragraph, and I'm not ready to give it up completely yet. In other cases I see a phrase or bit of dialogue that may come in handy somewhere else in the story—or in another story altogether. The challenge is figuring out how to file all of it so that I can locate that phrase when, months later, I find the perfect new home for it.

Take some time to think about balance. Are you trying to control the process, or are you learning to go with it? Are you developing your skill, mastering your craft, so that you can follow the creative flow and work with the material effectively?

Are you learning how to tap your creative flow and then let it bring what it will? Are you shifting into analytical mode when it's time and doing the work that needs to be done with the material?

Please note that the order of the process is not always the same. When I'm working on fiction, I'm usually free-writing first and then editing. When I'm working on nonfiction I'm often structuring the piece first and then tapping the creative flow as I fill in sections. You may be more of a left-brained thinker, someone who must always begin with structure and logic before you can allow the creative flow. The order doesn't matter as much as the presence of both processes.

The order of flow and analysis will also depend on your particular art. My husband, who is a photographer, considers that the most analytical part of his work is the shooting itself, which has to be technically on target to get the images in the first place. The more creative work is in the next stages—editing, cropping and applying digital adjustments. Even before photography went digital, Jim considered the more creative flow to happen within the editing rather than the shooting. Actors too must get the technical part before the creative flow can really kick in. Until you've memorized the lines, you can't do much with them. Only after you've determined how you're going to move your body during a scene can you allow the emotional energy to fill those movements. On the other hand, I talked with a painter who paints as much as I write—allowing the flow to spill onto the canvas and later coming back to edit by adding or scraping away.

Some kinds of balance will elude you in your creative life. But you are an active participant in this work, and while you cannot control the process, you can certainly become good at your work. You can become more adept at right-brained or left-brained work.

If you learn how to participate with the creative process so that you can perform both intuitive and analytical functions, you will finish more projects, and your skills will grow.

✒ EXERCISES FOR A WRITER'S FORMATION

Intuitive Work, Analytical Work

Make two lists. In one name as many tasks as you can that have to do with the more intuitive, right-brain aspect in your particular mode of creative work. In the other list, name all the analytical, left-brain tasks you can think of.

Now, on a large sheet of paper, try to draw a map of how your creative process works. Form a timeline and insert all the tasks from both columns where they seem to fall most of the time.

Brain Shift

Part 1: As quickly as you can, and without thinking about it, write a paragraph about the person who was your favorite relative when you were a kid. Write for just three minutes—anything you can think of.

Part 2: Now go back to that paragraph and rewrite it, only this time change something fundamental about the character. Change the gender, race or age category. Make the new paragraph of description fit this change.

Congratulations! In part one your work was intuitive, but you shifted to the analytical in order to do part two. In just a few minutes you have exercised both sides of your brain.

[A]t least in the actual act of writing, one has to be alone. That surely has nothing to do with community, and can only be stymied by it. Yet in leading my workshops, I have seen people stimulated by community while writing in the same room with others. Participants report a kind of group energy that raises the level of their own creativity, as they come to know one another through their mutual stories.

DAN WAKEFIELD, RELEASING THE CREATIVE SPIRIT

The individuality of a creator is not snuffed out in a mature, interdependent relationship. Rather, it is safeguarded there. It will take two people to accomplish this, two people who are walking separate paths and the same path together. The obstacles are enormous; yet the only question is, "Are you willing?"

ERIC MAISEL, THE VAN GOGH BLUES

When it comes to church there is an obvious conflict for the constitutional outsider who doesn't like belonging to organizations, hates the routine of having to be in the same place at the same time every week and finds it hard to fraternize with people who "don't understand." Yet lack of fellowship with a recognized body of Christians is the most common cause of artists loosening the moorings of their faith and then eventually becoming ineffective.

STEVE TURNER, IMAGINE: A VISION FOR CHRISTIANS IN THE ARTS

As writers we are always seeking support. First we should notice that we are already supported every moment. There is the earth below our feet and there is the air, filling our lungs and emptying them. We should begin from this when we need support. There is the sunlight coming through the window and the silence of the morning. Begin from these. Then turn to face a friend and feel how good it is when she says, "I love your work." Believe her as you believe the floor will hold you up, the chair will let you sit.

NATALIE GOLDBERG, WRITING DOWN THE BONES

6 THE COMMUNITY
THAT COUNTS

*When You Need Support
and Where to Find It*

I should confess that I come to the writing life with a distinct advantage: I've been editing other writers' work for about fourteen years. Day in and day out, finding the best place for this phrase, the accurate use of that word and the most effective organization for this chapter—all of this has taught me how much better a page of writing can be when it has been read and evaluated with care. Recently a publisher picked up my fourth novel, and when the editor asked me what I would need most from her in the editing stage, I said, "Once I turn it in, I want you to be merciless. I want every questionable word or phrase brought to my attention and every unclear paragraph brought into focus."

I have learned how to include community in my work because as an editor I am part of community for other writers. I give them instruction and encouragement, and I help them evaluate their strengths and weaknesses. As a writer I need this sort of assistance from my own editor. But editorial help is just one part of a writer's community. There are three categories of care that will likely be factors in your creative health: community, guidance and criticism.

❧ FINDING THE RIGHT COMMUNITY

As a Christian of several decades, I have formed a concept of community that is often at odds with the concept of the general culture around me. From my earliest days it was ingrained in my thinking—by Scriptures, hymns and liturgies—that we're all part of one community. The New Testament book of 1 Corinthians talks at length about what that means. I assume that if one person in my community suffers, all of us do. I believe that I share responsibility for the lives of people everywhere, if only through my prayers and my manner of life on this earth. I operate out of the worldview that I am irrevocably connected to other humans regardless of how well I know or like them, and vice versa.

In contrast, my culture would like me to believe that I can be a self-made woman, that if I make the right choices, purchase the right products and network with the right people I can "make it." I rarely get any message about self-sacrifice or commitment to my relationships (beyond legal bonds I enter willingly and upon the advice of an attorney) or my interdependence with anyone else. I grew up watching gold-tinted Westerns in which one person conquered the frontier or the bad guys or both.

And in the world of the arts, professional jealousy and the sense of a shrunken market almost guarantee that we carry on our work in isolation.

There are other reasons we so often create alone. Finding a healthy community in which to create is not always easy. Some religious communities especially are not particularly welcoming to people who are engaged in a creative process. And even communities that are not grounded in religion often won't get what creative people do.

Another reason we stay isolated is that we don't have a firm grasp ourselves of our creative process. Because we have not truly said yes to the work, or we haven't submitted to the process in an intentional way, or we haven't developed the practices we need, we are easily threatened by outside forces. When we're barely hanging on to a sense of our creative gifts, the last thing we want is to be thrust into a community that may or may not understand or help us develop them.

I think that community is probably a more difficult concept for young people who are just discovering their creative gifts. In the same way that youngsters often require a lot of private time to write in diaries, listen to music and just be with themselves, young artists probably need a lot of alone time in which to sort out what their gifts are and to discover what they need or want to say to the world. Solitude is necessary during certain periods of formation. I'll venture to state that young artists are usually self-absorbed, and this of course has to do with self-discovery as well as the lack of community. Such stages are probably necessary. I can remember how fearful and protective I once was concerning my creative work. When you are just developing your creative life, you can feel very fragile and unformed, and the presence of others—their opinions, their gifts and simply their distractions—can feel quite threatening. There are still stages during which I protect myself from outside interference while working on a project. So I don't judge the forming artist for apparent self-absorption. I respect the need for protection of one's gifts and thus the tendency of many artists to withdraw from human company. In the long-term arc of the creative life, however, community becomes crucial.

Gifts develop in community. They emerge from it and are energized by it. That doesn't mean that creative work evolves with people crowding around it. But it does mean that who you are as a creator is formed in the presence of other people. Your works come out of your interaction with those people. They may be family members or your Tai Chi class, or they may be your favorite essayists and painters, most of whom died a century ago. But you do have a community.

What Does Community Have to Do with Creativity?
You gather atmosphere from people you have known and still know. You glean ways of speaking, expressions of the face and hands. You pick up the emotional import of events and ideas from the people who

surround you. Your anecdotes come from others; your sense of urgency about important issues derives from public discourse about those issues. Your values and beliefs are connected to one subculture or another. Even your reactions against values and beliefs find their origin in whatever subculture you are reacting against.

Certain incidents in your history still influence your daily life; most of these incidents involve other people. Every time I make yeast bread from scratch, my father's presence visits me in some way, because my earliest connections to yeast bread came from watching him in the kitchen. I'd ask for a taste, and he'd pinch a bit of dough and plop it in front of me without interrupting the rhythm of his kneading. I can't make bread without some sense of Dad hovering around. Although Star Trek's *The Wrath of Khan* is one of my favorite movies, I can't watch it without remembering a very unpleasant summer when I roomed with a girl who was hostile toward me. The movie had just opened down the street, and I think I escaped our apartment three or four times to go watch *The Wrath of Khan* and thus avoid my roommate's unspoken wrath. I get irritated with my husband for taking corners too fast because at some formative point my grandmother commented that it was very rude to drive in such a way that passengers must shift in their seats to maintain balance. Many details of my speech and actions are marked by some past encounter.

You are marked in more ways than you'll ever recognize completely. The personalities and places within your past and present communities will pop up in your work whether you like it or not. Go ahead and find your quiet spot when you need to do your work, but embrace the frenzy around you otherwise. This is the life you draw from every day, for every work you create. These are the people who make up your environment, and you must know them if you are to delve into the meanings of that environment.

I have often regretted how inattentive I was while growing up in a small Midwestern town. It's amazing to me all the details I don't know about everyday life there. I was always cloistered, trying to be a writer, trying to survive my own forms of turmoil. And all the time farm seasons were going by, people were working on homes and machinery, in gardens and yards. They were having conversations and concocting entertainment. I missed a lot of it, mainly because I was fearful, something I learned from my religious subculture. But I was also an introvert and simply didn't understand at that time the importance of all those mundane details and everyday people.

Much of my daily community is beyond my choice or my control. I live in a city neighborhood, and I have extended family back in the Kansas farmland. I work for a company and belong to a faith community.

Then there is other community, that which I choose for myself, and much of that community I choose for how it helps my gifts. There is the community a person chooses for the sake of his or her artistic development.

How Do You Find a Community for Creativity?

Where do you find people who are good for you, who enhance your growth as an artist and who increase your confidence to keep up the work? For some people, a writer's group or some similar association works well. For others, a certain spiritual affiliation is most helpful, such as people from church or a small group from that faith community.

Some people find community primarily through others of like gifts—other artists. Sometimes it's enough to have close by the works of other artists. In the same way you might find spiritual companionship through the writings of C. S. Lewis or St. Teresa of Ávila, you can find creative company through the works of other artists, living or dead.

You can find community through a class where people like you hang out. You can find it through one or two good friends who can truly appreciate your work. You may not find community where you'd hoped; many artists are disappointed at how little community they find in their own family or in their religious organization. The point is to find it where it actually is and not to worry about where you don't find it.

The harsh truth is, many artists have fled "spirituality" because there was no room for them in their religious community. As long as their art fell within certain boundaries, they were considered okay. But of course creativity searches out the boundaries. Artists may explore a topic that is not considered safe; they use language and image that have not been used before in quite that way. They question the most sacred assumptions. Religious communities generally don't deal with these explorations in friendly ways.

So the young artist is guided away from using nude models. The young writer is chastised when her characters use profanity. The poet is called to account for a line that seems at face value to be quite antireligious. The playwright is given a story line to develop for worship purposes rather than trusted with her own story line.

In the beginning the criticisms come gently, as though the creative person merely needs a friendly reminder about what she should and should not be doing. But if she doesn't take heed, the warnings begin to lose their friendly feel. Given enough time, they turn into commands, censure and—eventually—rejection of the artist herself.

Many church systems don't know what to do with someone who is truly exploring the world. And certain Christian subcultures—I say Christian because this is what I know, not because I doubt that the tendency exists in other religions—are quite fearful of what cannot be cataloged, quantified, and put into terms of command and obedience. The fundamentalist culture I grew up in did not deal well with questions. If a person asked too many questions, she was seen as a problem child. I was too much of a conformist to fit that problem child category. It took me years to break away from the system and allow my art to be more honest. But I knew other creatives who simply left the church community rather than let it mess up their work.

As your creative work becomes more important to your whole life, you may have to make choices concerning your faith community. Some people are able to keep their work segregated in one part of their life and remain involved in a church community that is not particularly friendly to the work. They simply don't talk about their work when they are in their faith community. They keep it protected, away from judgment and censure.

For other folks, integration of creativity and spirituality requires that their spiritual community embrace and even approve their creative work. So they work at both sides until they find a fit, more or less. My creative work grew a lot when I was on the worship committee of an urban nondenominational church. That community welcomed artists and invited diversity in worship expression. I wrote twenty or more dramatic readings that opened up Scripture passages and biblical characters. At that time the two parts of my life lined up well. The faith community was hungry to experience fresh expressions of familiar themes, and I was ready to produce those fresh expressions. At the time I could do what I felt called to do without alienating my faith community.

But there were other periods during which I automatically censored myself in order to participate in faith community through my gifts. In those earlier years my faith development was probably more important than my freedom to stir up trouble on the creative front. Now I would not choose that sort of faith community because my creative work has become highly integrated with my faith. I find support through a few good friends who are also writers and artists. As it turns out, most of my artist friends are also people of active faith.

It's important to assess your situation honestly. Spiritual support of creative work may not come from your religious community. You may choose to stay with that community for many other good reasons. There's nothing wrong with that. Just keep looking until you find the community you need for your creativity. If it's a different community entirely, so be it. Many artists find their spiritual support with other artists.

"Community" doesn't have to be a large number either. One or two people who give you spiritual support on your creative journey can be more than enough. For years when I was younger, much of my support came from my grandmother. I got encouragement from teachers and my parents, but my grandmother always seemed to understand that the spiritual and creative were of one piece for me. In the early years she was all I needed. Now a few friends are all I need. I don't find it necessary to bring up my creative work in other contexts, because these friends support me as a spiritual as well as a creative person. Not all of them are Christian, but they respect my Christian faith and encourage me as I try to integrate that worldview with my storytelling.

As a teenager and college student, I used to feel that if a friendship did not evolve into a close relationship, it was a failure. Over time and many friendships I learned that a person has, if she's lucky, one or two close friends. Beyond that, she has not-so-close friends and more casual acquaintances. All of these relationships serve a purpose. I can enjoy acquaintances I see from time to time without suffering guilt because I'm not in better contact or don't share more confidences with them.

In the same way, I can enjoy Christian fellowship with people who would be upset if they knew more about my creative work. I'm not betraying anyone or anything by keeping those relationships separate from the work. I'm simply using good sense. I can participate in a faith community without revealing everything about my creative explorations. You don't tell every person your every secret. You don't burden every friend with your every struggle. And you don't reveal every twist and turn of your creative life to every person with whom you have some bond.

How Much Say Should Your Community Have in Your Creative Life?
If community is part of your creative life, then how much say are you giving others over what you create and how? Isn't this where censorship begins?

We can't really discuss censorship until we make some distinctions. There's creative work that the person produces in the course of artistic development, and there's creative work that is presented for public consumption. Sometimes a work will fit one but not both categories.

There are numerous reasons a particular work may not be put out there for others. For instance, it may contain a flaw or may not be quite up to standard.

Or it may be the wrong place and time to give it to the public. In chapter one I discussed the limitations a spiritual life may place on the creative life. Sometimes, for the sake of love, a creator will choose not to present a certain work to the public. For example, many memoirists wait until a parent has died before publishing the memoir that would have been hurtful to that parent. Other writers say, "It's my job to write it and publish it, and I can't be held back by those other considerations." Those writers are entitled to their opinion, and it's not for me to tell them otherwise. I live in the other camp, where considerations of the other become my considerations.

When Alice Walker's *The Color Purple* was adapted as a major film, it received a mixed reaction from the black community. There were those who felt that African Americans come under enough attack just for being black and that it wasn't right to deal publicly with sexual abuse in black families. Others, such as Oprah Winfrey, who acted in the film, thought it entirely appropriate to bring those sins to light. Two different opinions, each with its merit.

As a creative, you must not accept anyone's censure of what you produce. You follow your own process, because your process is generally wise and working for your benefit. You may paint dozens of dark, haunting pieces because you need to paint them. So much of what we do creatively is designed to help our own development. Think of how damaging it would be to tell a fourteen-year-old girl that she may write only happy things in her diary. What would be the point of a diary that presented only part of the story? Your creative work is in many ways your diary. It is how you process your own life. No one has the right to dictate your process.

You do have choices to make, however, concerning what works are appropriate for the community. Some works may be so intensely personal that they wouldn't connect with a larger audience anyway. Other works may emphasize the negative, providing a cathartic service, and those works would speak to people suffering the same demons as you—which is, in some situations, the very reason for displaying them publicly.

Whether or not a work makes a community angry or uncomfortable is beside the point. Often the purpose of art is to wake up communities, to make them face themselves. So I would never gauge a work's viability according to public reaction—which is rarely a thoughtful reaction.

There are several questions you ask of each work: Is this ready for the public? Have I taken the steps necessary to translate my experience so that it will speak to others? Have I considered who, if anyone, might be damaged by this work? Is this the right time to bring this topic into public discourse? Is this the right time in my own development to make this part of my life vulnerable to public discourse?

So there is a place for self-censorship, but generally it's not the censorship that the censors would apply. The best measuring stick is the artist's own judgment, and she must consider various factors.

Any community can decide what it will or will not support for public display. This is where democracy can do its work. In one community it may be inappropriate to display a given work of art because of how that work would be perceived. How many comedy groups use blackface makeup these days—a common device used in vaudeville of three generations ago? The American community, still struggling with racism, is generally not able to process this art form in a healthy way. It represents too much that has damaged us. If a tragedy happened in your town and it involved a certain object or song, would it be appropriate to use that object or song in a humorous way there just a few months later? The Nazi swastika is inappropriate in many settings because of its association with the Holocaust. It is entirely appropriate in other settings, according to its treatment. It's a powerful symbol of a particular kind of madness and evil, and some artists have used it as such.

Artists are often the very people who create new meanings from old symbols, but the transition phase, in the public view, can be quite difficult. That's not to say that the work shouldn't be created or displayed. The point is to use some discernment. A Christian worldview calls me to submit other judgments to the overarching purpose of love. Another artist without this worldview may not consider this a meaningful or necessary judgment. I believe that we should allow people the freedom to make their own judgments about what they should or should not present in public. Certainly politicians and lawmakers are not working from the intuitive wisdom that births creative works, especially disturbing creative works. I would tend to trust the artist more, because the artist is more likely to have a greater awareness and wisdom about the work. A maturing artist will also be tuned in to the community and its needs, because community connection is part of the creative process.

Some people make a passionate argument for "self-expression," but I don't think that art is about self-expression as much as it is about exploration and revelation. Exploration—even when it is, at a conscious level, self-exploration—will ultimately go beyond the self, in its drive to unveil the truth that is in the world. We cannot completely separate the self from the community or the environment. We were never meant to exist as a lot of autonomous beings. "Self-expression" is often merely an excuse for undisciplined art. When someone whines about self-expression, I don't have much empathy. I can more readily identify with a person who struggles with how a piece is evolving or who struggles to participate with the process and to develop personally through it.

There are no simple answers to the questions raised by censorship. This is all the more reason for creative people to develop their sense of community. We, of all people, can speak to our communities on an intuitive level—better than politicians and preachers can speak. And when we learn to be aware of the soul of our community, that wisdom can inform our work. We may still deliver disturbing messages, but they will be more likely to heal than to damage.

✒ FINDING THE RIGHT GUIDANCE

Everybody needs a helping hand, and most of us need the security of at least one person who is willing to walk a step or two ahead and help us on our journey. Pastors, therapists, spiritual directors, mentors, teachers and parents fill this role in various forms and at various times. Sometimes we need guidance over tough terrain, and other times all we really need is some company. But we cannot follow our calling in a vacuum. We need at least a person or two who can guide us where we've not yet been on our own.

The obvious forms of guidance are books, classes and instructors. These are helpful and sometimes necessary for the development of the craft. I have taken various creative writing courses, for the directed instruction and for the deadlines that forced me to complete projects. When I was teaching music in public school full time, I took a writing correspondence course that was helpful even though my only interaction was with the instructor who evaluated my assignments. Over time I also learned the value of peer review of my writing, and this is another excellent reason to participate in a class.

Books, classes and instructors are most effective for helping you with *craft*. You can't overestimate the value of learning well the nuts and bolts of your writing or painting or singing or gardening. If you don't learn the nuts and bolts, any inspiration will become more frustrating than helpful.

More subtle forms of guidance involve the mentoring that helps you with your creative life itself. You need not only the nuts and bolts but also the soul and the understanding that will help you thrive.

The tension of guidance in the creative life lies in the nature of creativity itself. Because creativity takes you where you haven't been, and because much of it emerges from your personal well, anyone who serves as a guide has got to do it without interfering. In various religious, educational and even professional traditions, "guidance" usually means that an authority figure explains the rules and then monitors to see who breaks them. Such guidance is fairly useless to the creative life. For one thing, another person can't dictate what the rules are for your creative work. It is yours alone; your Creator is quite willing to take you wherever you need to go, and that location may be uncomfortable for other people. But you need support. You need someone to walk alongside, not dictate the directions.

The guidance you need for your creative life is similar to the guidance a spiritual director gives. Spiritual directors are trained to pay attention to the person who's being directed. They are taught to get out of the way of what God is already doing in a person's life and to merely accompany the person on the journey. This is the guidance you need as a creative—guidance that gets out of the way while reflecting to you what you may not see clearly about yourself.

The best service your guide can offer is honest reflection of how you appear to be doing. A good guide will look to *you* for signals. Are you overburdened, taking on too much responsibility for the end result of this story or symphony or medical research? Are you fearful about something to the extent that you aren't free to follow the creative flow? Are you engaging in practices that are not good for you? Are you becoming overwhelmed by your creative endeavors? Are you avoiding honesty in your work? Are you avoiding *yourself* in your work?

At times you will need a person who carries the label of mentor or guide. At other times you'll find all the guidance you need in the company of one or two good friends who are invested in your development. For a year or so I met once every month with two other writers. They are both a few years older than me, and they tell me what I need to hear. For instance, one of them said concerning an essay I'd written, "The writing is fine—but *you're* not in here. When I really get engaged is when you're allowing your own story to enter, but then you cut it off, and I feel that you're leaving out the most important stuff." On the surface that was merely advice on writing. But what she was really getting at was that I was avoiding my own story. I was withholding the personal, and it was time to pay more attention to the personal. That's guidance. And because this person is also a friend who really cares about my development as a writer, her—and the other woman's—critiques of my writing will sometimes invoke assessment of how I'm doing in all of life.

The guidance you need as a creative is help with your life more than help with your craft. If your life is reasonably healthy, the craft will come with time and practice. You need mentors, fellow travelers, who will keep an eye on what your work is doing to you and for you.

A good mentor and fellow traveler is sensitive to what you need and when. And in order to be sensitive, a good mentor helps *you* express what you need.

You need someone who will question your motives sometimes. Are you writing this story because you feel that it will sell? Is there another story that's more important for you to write, never mind its marketability? You need people who will be accepting and forgiving when your writing is in a slump—when the characters aren't fully fleshed out and the themes are tired. We all go through such slumps, and sometimes we need to hear, "You'll pull out of this before long, and you'll get really interested in these characters again. Don't beat yourself up—just keep writing."

What do you need specifically from your mentor, and what can you find somewhere else? I get emotional support from my writer friends and from my husband. I get support for the deeper, more spiritual issues from my involvement in a faith community and occasionally from a therapist who is accepting of my spirituality and well acquainted with my history. I get more specific support for my writing life from my small circle of writer friends. I get technical help from a couple of editors I work with who are happy to read my work sometimes as freelance assignments. (They usually refuse to take money, because they're my friends, but I manage to pay them with food or some other reward.)

I suspect that it's best to find your guidance and support in more than one place. You don't want to put too much weight on a writing mentor; it may be best to get spiritual and emotional help somewhere else and reserve the energy of this mentoring relationship for the particulars of the writing craft. I wouldn't burden a mentoring relationship with the issues that my therapist helps me with so well. I would rather use a writing mentor's time and energy for helping my writing. And I rarely give my therapist something to read. What I need most from him is help in freeing my inner self to fully engage in my work.

What should you look for in a mentor, a person to accompany you on your creative journey? Here are some ideas, but this is certainly not an exhaustive list.

- Someone you get along with generally. You need to feel comfortable with this person.

- Someone who is not a major authority figure for you. The relationship will require honesty and vulnerability, and authority usually brings along a sense of judgment. So even if the person does not consider herself an authority over you, if you perceive her as such, that will stunt your ability to converse freely.

- Someone who is truly interested in your work and development. Feel free to pay good money to someone else for a professional review of your work. But your mentor should be engaging with you out of genuine care and interest.

- Someone who is a step or two ahead of you. You need a person who has journeyed a bit beyond you. If you seek guidance from a person who ends up getting advice from you more than the other way around, you will become frustrated and feel cheated.

- Someone who will not be threatened by your success. This is another reason to choose as a mentor someone who is already beyond you. A true mentor is rooting for you to do well and is the first person to jump up and down when you get published or win an award.

- Someone who has room for a little craziness. Creative life involves some craziness. Sometimes you need to go off on a tangent. Your mentor should understand that need and not get tied up in knots

when your creative work doesn't follow a straight line. A good
mentor will know when your craziness is necessary and when
you've begun to use it as an excuse not to focus on the work.

- Someone who is a good listener and observer. The best guide is a
  person who becomes very good at reading you. This person can reflect your soul back to you. In this sense your mentor becomes a
  sort of therapist. Avoid as a mentor someone who merely brings
  you books on writing or throws exercises at you and is constantly
  giving advice. You can find your own books. There are numerous
  books of writing exercises. In fact, books and exercises are what
  you take writing classes for. And advice is helpful only if it's what
  you need at the time. A good mentor will listen more than speak.

Assume that you will have different mentors at different times.
Your journey will call for specific means of help and encouragement
at each turn in the road. You may have one person who serves as sort
of a super-mentor for most of your life, but that is the exception more
than the rule. And if you're not investing every part of your life with
one person, it won't be so devastating when that person moves away
or becomes unavailable for other reasons. Mentors can come and go
just as friends do sometimes.

You may not feel the need for a mentor at all, or if so, rarely. I have
not sought out mentors but have enjoyed encouragement and feedback when they appeared. I am always on the lookout for other creative people who can journey with me, because the world is often a
strange place in which to dwell and do my work.

Some people just want to be left alone, and you may be one of
them. But do consider what you might gain at times from certain
kinds of guidance. Consider also what you may be missing by avoiding interaction with others who are invested in creative work.

FINDING THE RIGHT CRITICISM

You need criticism almost as much as you need encouragement.

Someone has to tell you what is in your work that hurts you or the work itself. You simply can't see the whole picture—ever—and you will never become objective enough to see your own work clearly. You've got to have discerning folk available who will give their honest opinions. Some of these people will be good friends, close enough that they will risk making you mad or hurting your feelings. Some of your best critics will be people who don't really care about you—they may not even like you or your project—but their experience and perception make their statements worth listening to.

There are some critics you should ignore—for instance, people who aren't qualified to give you advice. Some people have no credentials when it comes to the particular work you are presenting, and the gaps in their knowledge show because they get picky about the wrong things. They misread the purpose of the book, or they are seriously biased against the subject matter. Such reviews are not helpful, and at times they are mean-spirited. Ignore them, because they aren't helping you get better at your craft.

Years ago I heard a saying, and I don't remember who said it first. It went something like this. There are four types of people in the world: those who like you for the right reasons, those who like you for the wrong reasons, those who dislike you for the right reasons, and those who dislike you for the wrong reasons. The only people whose opinions should really matter to you are those in the third group: those who dislike you for the right reasons. So you should pay attention when people find problems in your work. You need to hear the truth that will help the process along, and sometimes that truth will hurt. Sometimes it will come from people who don't have any personal investment in you, but that's not the point. If they speak the truth, then you should pay attention.

It is important for our creative growth to get the right help at the right time. Sometimes we get the wrong help because we just don't know any better. I am often approached by young writers (young not necessarily in years but in experience) who think what they need is information about how to get published, when what they really need is training in the craft. I have to be honest and say that their writing shows giftedness but their craft is not developed enough for their work to be publishable.

Sometimes you will need help in devising practical ways to work with your gifts. You'll need ideas for creating practices and managing the logistics of your life to better accommodate your work.

Sometimes you will need a demanding course that will develop your technical expertise. I tell writers to take or audit courses in copyediting—a wonderful way to learn the intricacies of grammar.

One of the most crucial resources, however, is one of the least enjoyed. You need constructive criticism. And you need the right form of it at the right stage of any given work.

Whenever someone asks me to review something they've written, I ask, "What do you want from me, my general reaction or a ruthless line edit?" I can provide either, or something in between. But the person must tell me what she wants. This is important, because the wrong criticism at the wrong time can cripple the process.

Sometimes the feedback you want on a work is quite technical— you want someone to mark up the page and find your technical flaws. Usually this is in a later stage of the work, when you've done about all you can do for now. But such a detailed critique is not what you want in the earlier stages, when you are searching for the voice of a piece, when you're simply trying to locate the characters and their conflicts. Then you need a more general, intuitive kind of feedback. You need to know what part of the writing is the most emotionally engaging for the reader. You need to ask, "Do you care about this character, or am I using the wrong person as the protagonist?" You want to hear feedback such as "I think the story really starts on page five, and I'd like to hear more from the neighbor in the brick house. I think she may figure into this whole story more than you think."

Pay attention when other people don't understand what you're doing. Take note when they lose interest. As a writer, I know that when the reader gets bored, I have work to do; the scene isn't good yet if people are skimming past it. As an editor of prose, I know that any time I have to go back and reread a sentence or a paragraph or a page, there is a flaw in the writing. It could be an inconsistent verb tense or a modifying phrase in the wrong place. I encourage writers to pay attention to every mark an editor makes and every question she writes in the margins, because if she didn't understand the sentence, a lot of other readers won't either. When you learn to pay attention to criticism, you will grow in your craft. You may not take every suggestion offered, and you shouldn't, but a question is usually a red flag.

I tell writers whose work I edit that they should allow themselves a curse-and-cry period. This is after they receive the edited manuscript back from me. You're never truly prepared for that marked-up manuscript. You're immediately mad and crushed when you see all the things either that you didn't do right or that this stupid reader didn't understand. Criticism always hurts at some level. So let it hurt. Cry and throw things—I do—and then after you've vented and can calm down, go back and look at every mark and ask yourself each time if there's any merit at all to this correction or question. So far in my writing career, I've agreed with about 95 percent of the corrections and comments made by editors. They get paid for editing because they are skilled to help people with word crafting. So when you turn to another craftsperson for help, get ready to accept what's offered.

Get into classes and other forums that allow for healthy criticism. A good facilitator won't permit bashing and will require that any critic back up the criticism rather than just spout opinion. I'm forever grateful for the few creative writing courses I've attended that built in real criticism from both teachers and peers. It stings when people find flaws in your work, but it's really amazing how improved your efforts will be after you've worked with those problem spots and applied some of the advice offered to you.

Following is an outline I use when preparing writers to critique one another. This outline breaks down the type of feedback according to the stage of the work. Of course this applies specifically to writing, but it can give you some ideas for how you might outline forms of critique for other kinds of creative work.

At every stage, ask these two questions:

- Who is the audience?
- What is the genre/format?

Early Stage: Forming the Idea

When a work is in the early stages, you don't want input that will interfere with the formation. For instance, you don't turn over an early draft to someone and ask him or her to go over it with a red pen. Early draft is not the time for corrections to grammar and sentence structure. There's a chance you will totally rewrite the piece anyway and eliminate the troublesome sentence or the phrase that doesn't work. A thorough, technical critique at this point will merely frustrate you.

So in the early stage, talk about the general idea. If you do hand over an early-draft passage from this work-to-be, ask these sorts of questions:

- What's your general emotional reaction to this idea?
- Is it interesting?
- Where are you most emotionally engaged?
- What do you think the point is, or where do you think it's going?
- Where do you want more?
- Where do you want less?

Intermediate Stage: Putting It Together

Once the idea is pretty solid and you've produced quite a bit of raw material, it's time to start shaping the piece. The intermediate stage will probably involve a lot of rewriting, filling in passages and rearranging material. Because it's a time of revision, you can afford to ask more dangerous questions:

- Is it easy to follow, or are there places where I lose you?
- Where do I need to provide more information?
- Where do I need to trim some fat and provide less information?
- Does the tone welcome you? Does it put you off in any way?
- Is it compelling?
- At what point does your interest flag?
- Have I found the right beginning/end?

Final Stage: Fixing It

When you're in the final stage, you've done about all you can do. You have rewritten, restructured, rethought and reimagined this piece. You have checked the spelling, grammar and other technical aspects. And at this point you are probably sick to death of this thing.

It's time to call in someone who will now be more ruthless than you have the objectivity to be. Now any red mark is fair. When you turn over a work for this type of critique, it's usually good to say, "I'm taking two weeks off from this, so take your time and mark it carefully, but don't call me in the meantime." This final-stage critique is the perfect opportunity for you to take a long-needed rest and to not think about the work. While you're getting some R&R, your critic will be evaluating the following:

- tone
- pacing
- emotional engagement
- sentence structure
- grammar
- spelling
- transitions
- anything that jars the reader
- anything that doesn't flow well or that is unclear
- tension/release

- promise/delivery
- good on the ear?
- author tics

"Author tics" is my term to describe the mistakes that are common to a particular author. For instance, before I turn over any written piece for publication, I do a search for any form of the word *actual*. For some nutty reason I have fallen in love with this word, and I use it and use it. I have learned to seek and destroy it in everything I write. I have other bad habits too, as does any writer or other artist. After a while you will become acquainted with your own tics and can do as I do— make a special check for them. But sure as you unlearn one habit, a new one will develop to take its place. So your critic should be free to point out these tics to you.

As you may have noticed, the more developed the piece, the more specific and craft-related should be the critique; the more unformed the piece, the more general and nontechnical should be the critique. Don't invite final-stage criticism on an early-stage piece, because it will devastate you and possibly stop the work altogether. And don't give a final-stage work to a critic and list all the things he or she can't criticize, because a soft, general critique at the end is worthless and will not help you make the piece as good as it can be.

When I open up my work to another person's judgment, I feel about as vulnerable as I ever feel, outside of a doctor's examining room. At this point I've published a number of books, and even now when I send a manuscript off to the editor, a part of me goes into hiding, fearful of all the flaws that will be revealed in my little masterpiece. When I get the manuscript back, all marked up, a stone drops to the bottom of my stomach. *What? I'm not perfect? I made errors?* I give myself an afternoon or a day to be upset and discouraged. Then I get to work.

I recall when the proofs of my first novel came back for my review. I was on a business trip, in a hotel room for the weekend. When I wasn't in meetings I was back in the room slogging through all the comments and questions, finding mistakes that I couldn't believe I hadn't caught earlier. I threw a pillow or two and wailed over the phone to my husband. But I was so grateful for the people who had come after me, examining the work and flagging the problem spots. By the end of the weekend I'd made the repairs and dried my tears.

What a process, this writing life. If my gifts didn't lead me here, I'd be an idiot to ever get involved with it. Thank goodness I don't have to do it alone.

✍ EXERCISES FOR A WRITER'S FORMATION

The Right Community

Describe the communities you have been part of throughout your life. Be specific about how those communities have interacted with your creative gifts.

How could you have been better supported in your creativity?

Who encouraged your gifts the most, and how did he or she do that?

What kind of community do you now have in relation to your gifts?

Write a paragraph or two, completing this thought:
The community I want to create for myself and my gifts will be possible only if . . .

The Right Guidance

Complete these thoughts:

The support I need for learning my craft is _____, and this is how I will go about finding that support:

The help I need emotionally and spiritually would best be described as _____, and this is a step I will take toward finding that help:

The Right Criticism

Complete these statements.

The criticism I most fear getting is . . .

I remember a time when I didn't listen to criticism that would have helped me, and the result was . . .

I also remember a time when someone gave me criticism that was totally unhelpful. As I look back on it, I realize that this happened because . . .

Being attached to a specific outcome at the beginning prevents order from emerging through the creative process. Likewise, when the self-interested ego convinces us that its kind of security is essential to our well-being, it prevents us from exploring what our soul really needs.

REGINA COUPAR, THE ART OF SOUL

And so story helped me to learn to live. Story was in no way an evasion of life, but a way of living life creatively instead of fearfully.

MADELEINE L'ENGLE, WALKING ON WATER

We are all under the same mental calamity; we have all forgotten our names. We have all forgotten what we really are. All that we call common sense and rationality and practicality and positivism only means that for certain dead levels of our life we forget that we have forgotten. All that we call spirit and art and ecstasy only means that for one awful instant we remember that we forget.

G. K. CHESTERTON, QUOTED IN THE CHRISTIAN IMAGINATION:
G. K. CHESTERTON ON THE ARTS

What is it you wanted to say? What do you want to expose about yourself? Being naked in a piece is a loss of control. This is good. We're not in control anyway. People see you as you are. Sometimes we expose ourselves before we understand what we have done. That's hard, but even more painful is to freeze up and expose nothing. Plus freezing up makes for terrible writing.

NATALIE GOLDBERG, WRITING DOWN THE BONES

In large measure becoming an artist consists of learning to accept yourself, which makes your work personal, and in following your own voice, which makes your work distinctive.

DAVID BAYLES AND TED ORLAND, ART AND FEAR

7 THE SELF YOU MUST FACE

Where Your Gifts Begin and Where You Must Return

I've been writing a book of memoir-essays for at least three years. The first set seemed pretty good, but the feedback I got from writer friends was lukewarm, so I took that as a sign that they weren't ready. I went back to them a year later and thanked God for honest friends; the writing was stiff, and I had barely engaged with most of the topics.

So I had another go at it; I think the second draft is what I sent to my agent. She was encouraging but said, "Let's keep this on the back burner for now." That was fine; I had other projects in the works, and by then I sensed that the essays might be the toughest project I'd ever taken on.

When I approached them for the third or fourth time, I recognized the biggest flaw: I was trying to come to some sort of philosophical closure on matters that were deeply personal. And while the philosophy can be helpful and, when written artfully, satisfying to read, what readers really want is the story.

Well, I'm not that intrigued by my own story, and I have a long-standing fear of self-absorption, which can really kill good writing. So

I've said all along, "I don't think my story merits much attention. This is why I write novels; I can create characters who are far more interesting." Yet the essays would not let me go. I kept returning to them, and every time I wrote them, they opened up a little more.

Each time I rewrote an essay, my story came forward a little more, my history opened a bit wider, and I became more visible. This was not comforting.

However, I finally gave in a few months ago and began to write from the most honest place I could find. I began to write about the fears I'd always been embarrassed to share, the little obsessions that reveal me as just a human being after all, one not very wise at all, who is too small and unformed herself to stand at the front of the room and formulate a philosophical approach to life.

When I turned in the new version of the introduction, my agent responded that it was exactly right, and I uttered some mild profanity. Okay, this is my life, and I suppose that if I write essays, I will need to let others see this life, really see it. I come to the writing every other week or so for maybe an hour. It is uncomfortable work, but my gut tells me that it's the right work. There are stories in my soul, and they are the ones that count the most.

Your soul has been spinning stories since the day you were born. And those stories are not yours alone. They belong to your parents and ancestors. They belong to your hometown and region of the country. They are best told in their original dialect, and only someone from the area can do that successfully.

Your creativity is likely to thrive and be especially productive when you are willing to face your life at many levels, understand your roots and embrace yourself in the most intimate ways. This doesn't mean that all of your creative work will be about you. But its power and relevance come from your well. Sooner or later you must go home again. You must face the depths of that well. The parentage, the family story, the tribal story, the story of the hometown or region—all of it contributes to who you are now. We transplanted white Europeans don't have much sense about this. Native Americans on the whole have always understood the importance of place and history and how those things manifest in a single life. Many African Americans have relearned the importance of their deeper roots for overcoming the legacy of slavery. When Alex Haley published *Roots* back in 1976, he was saying to generations of black people in America, "Your story began *before* the slavery—and it's a rich and wonderful story indeed."

For all of us, there is a deeper story. And we creatives do well to pay attention to it. We are wise to dive into the well, even though it can be a scary proposition.

ACCEPTING YOUR HISTORY

During the 1990s memoir came back into fashion. Suddenly a whole lot of baby boomers began to face up to their own histories and write about them. I'm sure this happened because boomers hit midlife and began asking the big questions concerning their reasons for living and what they might leave as a legacy. And these books have sold reasonably well, because a lot of other boomers were attracted to the authors' midlife search for meaning. I'm at the tail end of the boomer generation, and since hitting age forty a few years ago, I've needed to do more summing up than seems normal or even healthy. But it's a stage I must pass through, so I write what I can.

Well-written memoir provides good role modeling for creative people. There's nothing more fascinating than a person's life story, once the person has processed it well enough to write about it in an unselfconscious way, once he or she is able to write the bigger picture that contains the personal picture. A good memoirist has managed to do what all artists must eventually do: face personal history in a reasonably mature way. Such confrontation must go several steps further than mere therapy, further than simply stating all that has been wrong in one's life, further than tapping pain and anger at what has been brutally true or false. Such confrontation is soul work, and when it is done well the results are healing and wisdom—and mighty fine art.

But aren't beginnings meant to be left behind, overcome, moved beyond? Many of us run away from our beginnings as far and as fast as we can, because we sense the damage or the danger. It is considered good mental health to move beyond the former abuse, neglect, grief or oppression. Likewise, mature art escapes the former naiveté or simplicity in order to explore life's dark complexities.

There is a difference between moving beyond origins and rejecting an important part of yourself. It's useless to run from your origins, because they are the roots of your soul, and you cannot dismiss them without dismissing something fundamental about yourself. Perhaps you have finally left the prison of a horribly dysfunctional family system; your life is healthier now, and you are certainly freer to pursue your life callings, including your creative callings. Each of us must grow up and beyond our childhood self. But those roots will continue to produce little shoots in your life. Until you deal with them very bluntly, you risk becoming the propagator of the same ills and imbalances that were visited upon you. And your creative work will contain strange gaps—places where important information is obviously missing.

The aspects of your personal history that you want to avoid can be the source of great vision for you. If you leave out something that has wounded you deeply, others will sense the hole in your story. This doesn't mean that you have to turn your every wound and shame into a work of art. It simply means that eventually you must deal with the wounds and the shame. You have to move from being a victim to becoming a creator. Everything in your life—good and bad—can be raw material for your wisdom and creative skill. And you learn the most from your toughest struggles.

I've come to believe that artists are given the task of healing their culture through their explorations, through their renaming and revisioning of events. It is part of my gift as a writer to unveil the wisdom and redemption within difficult times, to name things accurately so that my community can face the truth about itself. I begin this service by facing the truth about my own story.

Anything that disturbs my soul will disrupt my creative work as well. In fact, creative work will often lead me to healing, because it will direct me to deal with what is hurting my soul. Because of this, many artists grow spiritually and emotionally through, rather than in spite of, their art.

For a long time I wished that I could have grown up in some college professor's house, surrounded by intellectuals and artists, versed in all the "classics" and trained to label things appropriately. My gifts drew me toward study and art, but I came from a blue-collar family, descended primarily from farmers and coal miners. We lived in a little town surrounded by soybeans and wheat. Rather than jazz, there were Baptist hymns. Rather than the great Impressionist painters, there was Currier and Ives. My parents and grandparents were well read, and they made sure I had good books from an early age. But my context did not turn me into the person I wished I had become by the time I was in college and rubbing shoulders with the offspring of more "cultured" people.

I was in my mid-thirties and had lived in cities for a while before I dared to think more kindly of my origins. I began to listen more intently to my grandmothers' stories. I ventured to study my hometown when I was there for visits. And I began to write fiction, which of course was set in a fictitious town that was actually that hometown. People began to emerge, people I discovered that I loved very much. I wanted to know them better. So I put them into stories and I let them speak to me.

When that first book was published, one of the most passionate responses I received was from a man who also had come from small-town beginnings. He said, "Your book made me want to go back to my hometown and get to know all those people I ran away from, years ago." So I had tapped something important, not only for me but for others too.

There are still aspects of my origins—childhood illness, early deaths of relatives, my family's brand of dysfunction—that require great patience on my part. Sometimes they require forgiveness. I am not obligated to call them anything but what they are. But I have reached a point of acceptance—at least about some matters—that has freed me to get on with my life and with other stories. I've lived in Chicago long enough that I expect to set an upcoming novel not in a little Kansas town but in a city. I'm not sure I could write of cities, though, had I not first returned to the little town.

Your origins might be delightful—or they might be filled with horror. Give them the names they deserve, but work at facing them. You may not turn them into stories or paintings, but you can use them for the sake of wisdom and your own freedom. As long as you avoid and hate them, great energy is required to maintain that distance and hatred. Once you have looked at your origins head-on, called them what you would and accepted their existence in your life, you will have more liberty to pursue whatever comes next.

Understand why you are who you are. One of the greatest resources you have for studying human nature is your own history. Delve into the family stories. Trace patterns of behavior or similarities of personality from one generation to the next. Do a family tree. Draw a family timeline that includes important events for the past several generations. Look for the characters that gave the family its reputation. Look for the decisions that made substantial impact on the family's direction. Look for the livelihoods that hurt or helped, at the childhood traumas that shaped the adults. I promise that within your family alone is enough material to fuel half a lifetime of creative works.

Understanding your history will also reveal important keys to your own traits and preferences. Pay attention when Great-Aunt Della comments that you remind her of so-and-so. Ask why. So-and-so may offer some insight about why you operate as you do. Ask about the illnesses that have plagued the family; was there undiagnosed depression, a series of miscarriages, a run of cancer? Did the environment play a part, such as the black lung that killed Great-Granddad or the chemical refuse that poisoned the stream on the family property? As you look back at the health history, do you find changes that might still make a difference to the current and future generations? When you realize that there's a history of bipolar disease, could that matter to the cousin who is just now struggling with serious depression? These questions open up all sorts of scenarios. They also give you important information, not only for your creative life but for life in general. Sometimes the searching you do for creative purposes can bring wisdom that wasn't so apparent before. Sometimes by simply piecing together your family history, you can offer some benefit to people still in the family.

Once you've dealt with the more obvious issues, such as physical health, try deeper questions: What have been the driving fears and desires in this family? What fears rearranged the way people did things or where they lived? What desires gave them courage to start a new career or adopt a child?

One set of questions will lead to whole other sets of questions. One strand of material will engage with another. And all of it's an education about how people work, how families function, how systems evolve and get dismantled.

This is soul work. It matters a lot, because that history has resulted in you, the person. When you dip into your well for your stories or whatever your creative work is, this history—however fragmented or reinterpreted—is what you'll find. You can't dip up anyone else's history. You can spend years in research, live in another subculture, acquire a Ph.D. studying about other people's wells and collect hours of interviews about others' lives. But you will never be able to draw up the stories that reside in other people's wells. And other people will never be able to draw up your stories, because they are for you alone—your perspective, your traits and your experience.

≈ EMBRACING YOUR PERSONALITY

This is a tough one. At least for some of us, it's very tough. Much of my introverted life has been socially awkward. Between my personality and others' reaction to it, as a youngster I was steeped in negativity.

It was painfully difficult to talk with people. I was generally fearful of new people and unfamiliar situations. I hated being put on the spot— one reason I always detested playing games, which felt to me like forced interaction. I was never sure how to dress or walk or talk.

I was ill a lot as a child and thus held back from the tomboyish activity that would have expressed my true nature. I was skinny and nervous from an overactive thyroid, then medicated several years to the point of developing numerous health complications in reaction to the medication. During early childhood I had been interested in sports, but my condition prevented any athletic achievement and in fact made me wary of anything suggesting a need for physical coordination or strength. To this day sporting events are foreign and intimidating to me.

My only salvation was that I was smart and liked to please authority, which meant that my academic career was stellar from the word go. This gave me some sense of achievement, but it did nothing for my social life, or for the social life that might have been. Not only was I awkward and sick-looking, I made better grades than everyone else. These attributes do not a popular child make.

During adolescence I found a larger salvation, in Jesus, and thus began an intense career in religion, which only further alienated me from normal people. By then my creativity, thank God, had begun to bloom, and I was preoccupied with writing, singing and playing piano. Much of the time these minivocations kept me from feeling the absence of normal things such as hanging out with other kids, learning to dress or use makeup, listening to the radio or navigating relationships with the opposite sex. Of course I had no dating life.

Every person has her own personality to face, and no one is totally comfortable with what she perceives herself to be. She is too shy, or she talks too much. She threatens men or is manipulated by them. She can never find clothes to fit. She can't seem to maintain healthy friendships. She can't stick to one thing until it's finished. We each have a laundry list of what we would change if only we could. Some of us go to great lengths to change what we can, whether by cosmetic surgery or by a complete about-face in career or religion.

Unfortunately—or maybe fortunately—the basic person stays the same. We can dress her differently, teach her a new language, force upon her different habits and charms, but she will remain essentially who she is.

After all this time, I'm just too tired to obsess about the flaws in my person. On some days I still go on a rant about what my body is doing (i.e., aging) without my permission. Or I will fume at my husband for wounds in my woman self for which he is not even responsible. But those are the really bad days. After all this time, I have become better acquainted with the flaws in other people, and I've decided that we're all struggling. And most of us are so busy with our personal struggles that we are fairly unaware of how others don't measure up.

In fact, for every dark side of your personality there is the lit-up side. There is the strength you have now because you endured other kids picking on you, or there's the empathy you carry for others who suffer from being overweight or from speech impediments. There's also the ability to step outside of yourself when necessary, something you learned during those periods when being you was just too painful. You've learned to adjust to your own messed-up nature; thus you are well equipped to adjust to other people too. If you're lucky, you've learned to forgive yourself, and you can't get too much practice at forgiveness.

By studying yourself, flaws and all, you are better prepared to study others. You are better able to take a character apart and build an entire plot out of one neurosis. When you unveil your own ugliness, your vision will increase. And you have acquired yet another filter through which to observe life. You know what it means to feel alienated, so bring that to life in this painting or song. You know how it feels to be trapped in a personality that just won't straighten up, so create an atmosphere from that.

I have come to more acceptance of my lopsided self in the last decade or so. I know that everyone else is lopsided too and that to aim for perfect balance is a waste of time. I have my own flaws to overcome, my own patches of darkness to handle. Dealing with those matters is simply part of my job as a person.

At the same time, I see how the very personality I abhorred for so long has developed incredible abilities of perception. If I had been a rowdy participant during those childhood years, would I have evolved into this writer, this unobtrusive absorber of sights and sounds? Would I have worked so hard to understand things if life had been easier for me? Would I have pursued my creative work if I'd been the life of the party and had a date every weekend? I don't think so. I think I could have been seduced away from my soul work had my life setting been more comfortable and my personal space less complicated. So although I am still haunted by memories of pain—as a child, an adolescent, a college student, a young adult—I'm fairly pleased with the adult I've become. And I would not be this person had I not been all the others first.

Embrace your personality. Study it, love it, exploit it to the fullest. Find the angles that are specifically yours, and work from them. There are stories only you can tell, because they are intrinsically tied to who you are and who you have been. Keep working on the flaws, the weaknesses, the neuroses. But do it with love. You are just a person, after all, in need of help, in need of a friendly place to live. You are probably already your own worst enemy; it's time to learn how to be your own best friend. No one else can do the job any better.

✎ UNDERSTANDING YOUR PHYSICAL LIFE

Awareness of your body will help you maintain a better balance in other areas of life. Many of our problems become more manageable when we're rested and eating well. We're in a better mode to create when our physical systems are healthy. And when we face who we are physically, we're better able to create art that presents the whole person and appeals to more than an audience's ideas and beliefs.

I address sexuality in three different chapters of this book. I'm not obsessed with sex, but I am convinced that a general avoidance of sexuality cripples artistic expression time and time again. So I bring it up here in the context of facing yourself. Your sexuality is at the heart of who you are, and it will figure into your creative work one way or the other.

Sex has to do with everything. The sooner we accept this, the better everything will go. Our avoidance of sexuality has cost us more than can ever be calculated. It is the huge, purple elephant standing in the middle of the room that nobody talks about. Well, we do talk about it, but not in a helpful way. Sexual issues quickly become polarized and demand that people choose sides and get argumentative. We talk about sex in order to get the upper hand, in order to gain some kind of control over it. How much better we would function if we could at least talk about sex in normal tones of voice.

My husband, being a photographer, and I, being a writer, enjoy observing life together. Thanks to our many discussions, I've learned to approach the world more visually and he more verbally. We were at an Italian eatery a couple of years ago, and the waitress looked like another Sophia Loren waiting to happen. Jim and I discussed the particulars of her beauty. She wasn't dressed immodestly, and she wasn't flirting. But her sexuality was the young, vibrant kind, and it was a pleasure to witness it. By discussing it as we did, we gave sexuality its proper place. We approached it as an important part of life, important enough to merit our attention and our praise. We have just as enthusiastically observed and discussed exuberant toddlers in church, the changing colors of Lake Michigan and a particularly creative series of vodka advertisements. Why discuss freely so many things and yet grow silent about the most natural chemistry in human nature?

We are hungry for physical contact. We were made this way. Much of sexuality has to do simply with being touched. In fact, if we were more comfortable with nonsexual physical contact, we would be less likely to fall into inappropriate sexual activity. Because sex is a matter of the spirit, what we're reaching for when we get involved with someone sexually goes far beyond the physical activity. It has more to do with connecting with another person, with feeling wanted, attractive and worthy of love. Our creative gifts offer us ways to connect, to express beauty and to recognize our own significance; thus they can meet many of the needs that we often associate with an act of sex.

I have learned to admire beauty wherever I find it, and that means that I can enjoy the sight of beautiful people without turning that joy into sexual preoccupation. One day as I was riding the commuter train, a handsome man walked on and sat down, and I admired his beauty from my place several seats away. Then it occurred to me that not only was this man quite beautiful to behold but the woman sitting on the other side of the train was lovely as well. So was the older gentlemen over there. And the young immigrant father and his toddler daughter. In a matter of moments, every person on that train car had become, in my eyes, extraordinary and beautiful. It all began because an attractive man walked onto the train. If I had been so afraid of sexuality that I averted my eyes, would my heart have opened up to all those other people?

I've been married for more than a dozen years now, and I'm surprised that more people don't explore through art the power of married sexual expression. Maybe it's not perceived to be as exciting as extramarital sex, but the marital relationship informs all aspects of life. When the relationship extends over years, the wisdom and wonder of it deepen. Perhaps artists don't explore it much because it could easily impinge on their privacy—after all, even if the scenes don't come from the writer's own marriage, people might assume that they do. But those of us who believe that marriage is good and sacred should find more ways to express its beauties. Wouldn't it be refreshing to see a film about a marriage getting better, even through conflict and disappointment, rather than the tired plot in which one spouse leaves the other for a newer, "easier" coupling? And aren't we satisfied deep down when we meet a truly happy couple celebrating thirty or fifty years together? The world needs compelling expressions of this foundational relationship.

Better that you look steadfastly at the wonder of sexuality, write about it and enjoy it than refuse to acknowledge it at all. Many people are still far more sexually repressed than they realize or will admit. Of course they get upset when the artists among them awaken to human sexuality and want to express that in their work. But artists should explore all of life, not just the flowers and sunsets. Spiritual people must stop neutering themselves by making sexuality an evil thing that can and must be locked away from the rest of life.

At the same time, the artist must discern what the current work requires and what could be simply tacked on for other reasons. Further, we have to consider how we will communicate to people who are numbed by a culture that simplifies and exploits everything. I am writing a novel now in which a wife has an affair, and I am asking myself how much of the sexual involvement needs to be written. Some of it must be there, because I am trying to show how powerful this attraction has become. I am exploring why a married woman would do this and how it would feel once she's taken such a drastic step. So some of the scenes will have to explore her sexual reactions and situations. But I must also ask myself if I am looking for a way to include sex scenes because readers expect them. At what point is it a compromise? I have no problem with writing a sex scene if the development of the story calls for it. But I need to figure out when it is called for as opposed to when I feel pressured by my culture to include it.

It's important for creative people to tackle sexual themes, because that is the only way our communities will learn to deal with those themes honestly. If we don't include sexuality in our material, we are merely contributing to the ignorance and fear that pervade our world. If a skilled novelist won't help her readers explore what it means to be faithful or unfaithful, who will? Preachers? Usually the only people who listen to preachers are the people who already agree with the preachers. Who better than a songwriter or painter to help people face their own passions? Songs and images reach passions faster and with much more force than do the speeches of politicians or moralizers. Art that is well conceived looks at a situation honestly and explores an idea in depth, which is more than will ever be accomplished by a motivational talk or a sound bite.

We can complain about how shallow the culture is. Or we can contribute to that culture works of creativity that will help people stop and thoughtfully consider the complicated struggles that are important to them.

◈ USING YOUR EXPERIENCE

I'm a book editor who works for a publisher, and this is one field in which hardly anybody is doing what she got a college degree to do. We were teachers first, or musicians, or on a church staff, or professionals at something else. Our degrees are in history or statistics or accounting or special education. There are few degrees or university programs in publishing. So most of us get into this business through career detours.

Many people who are past their mid-twenties have already shifted careers at least once. We end up in a job that is barely related to our degree or our original plans. Among people who enter artistic fields, it's almost a certainty that we are able to do our creative work precisely because we've also had a string of "day jobs." Artists deal with the ongoing tension between doing their creative work and putting in hours at other work in order to afford the creative work. I joke about keeping my editing job to support my writing habit.

This can feel like a severe disadvantage, never being in a position to quit all work except for your creative endeavors. But creative work is fed by any and all experience. Perhaps there's a cosmic reason that artists have always needed either benefactors or a long series of various jobs. If all I do is write, what can I write about? What better keeps me in the flow of people and events than having to drag myself to a regular job X number of hours per week?

Everything that happens to you stores up life experience. Everything you do, whether you feel like it or not, fills your well with worthy material. I get nervous around writers who spend forty hours a week at the computer and have ceased to be out among the crowds, doing everyday things, facing normal inconveniences and conflicts. As much as I may daydream about holing up in a cabin on Michigan's Upper Peninsula, stocked with enough food and drink to last two or three months, spending days on end spinning my fiction, I know that the reality would not be so pleasant. Even now I write an hour or two and then have to do laundry or grocery shop—anything to get my body moving and to air out my thoughts. And if my eyes and ears are open at all, I encounter material for my storytelling even as I wander the aisles of the produce store.

All experience counts. When I was a kid, we always had a couple of dogs that stayed in our yard for the most part but also wandered the neighborhood—this was normal in rural towns. They were "town dogs," and unless they turned mean or destructive, nobody worried about their being loose. One elderly neighbor, a sort of busybody who lived in the house across the alley from us, complained once to my dad that our dog had "done his business" in her yard. To folks in the country, a pile of dog poop is not a big deal. My dad just laughed at this exchange, and it never came to anything, just a blip in small-town life. This lady had known Dad since he was a little brat. She probably was complaining just to have somebody to talk to.

For some reason I remembered that bothersome pile of dog poop. And I gave to one of my key characters, Mamie Rupert, an old neighbor whose dog has chosen Mamie's carefully landscaped yard as his morning toilet. This becomes a major issue in Mamie's life, setting her full of desire that generates more energy than she's had in twenty years. The dog business is key in a great religious scene of Mamie's story. And it provides genuine humor. People love the bit about Mamie and the dog poop.

I couldn't have sat down and thought up something like that. All I had was that brief scene between Dad and the neighbor from years ago. Never discount any experience, large or small, ugly or not. You'll be surprised at the tidbits you'll find in the well, the leftover pieces of life's drama that never amounted to much in the actual experience but that open up surprising possibilities in your work.

In that same novel I used my own fear of water to make vivid how depression feels to a teenage boy. It is one of the best descriptions in the book, because it plays on the very tangible feelings of being in water that's too deep when you don't know how to swim. It is the perfect metaphor for someone slipping deeper into something that's outside of his control, of being forced by outside pressure toward something he really doesn't want. It wasn't difficult to come up with a paragraph drawing on my own experiences of being in public swimming pools and finding myself in deeper water than I could handle. Experience: just a small but meaningful slice can make all the difference.

The glory of experience is that you can cut it to ribbons and use only what you care to use. I used the sensation of being in deep water, not an entire episode of going swimming with friends. I used dog poop and an old lady, and I used it quite differently from how the actual conflict had played out. You use portions of scenes, fragments of conversations, flashes of emotion. You do whatever you want with it. You keep a face but change a gender, keep a landmark but change the time of year, keep a job description but change the personality of the supervisor. In fact, you must change enough to remove it from real people and events, for liability reasons. But you need to change it anyway, because it's material that you shape and situate according to your own purposes.

I have lost a father to diabetes. I've lost a child to miscarriage. I've nearly lost a husband to depression. I've lost siblings to distance, friends to changes of faith and faith to changes of life. My losses all count as experience. I don't know when I'll use any of it, but one day I will need to remember what it felt like to lose each of these, because a character in a story will need to go through something like that, and it's my job to make the story tangible to the reader. I fill up the spaces between the words with the essence of my own memories and experiences. It's a marvelous system, because nothing is wasted. Grief is not wasted, long years of waiting are not wasted, physical pain is not wasted. Even depression is not wasted. Recently I chose not to medicate a particular bout of depression. We (my husband, my therapist and I) determined that it was not a dangerous depression, mainly an experience akin to walking through fog. Low energy, low desire, a flatness of emotion—but I could function more or less. I decided to simply live in this state, to write about it and study it while it happened to me. If it had lasted weeks and weeks, or if it had degenerated into suicidal hopelessness, we would have responded more aggressively. But this time it seemed wise to do nothing.

I studied and lived this depression for more than two months. My productivity was cut nearly in half. My writing nearly stopped altogether. But I gathered information about my interior life, about how it hooks into larger, harder life. I did some writing—not much, but enough—to help me recall later with great clarity what it is like to have no energy and no desire, what it is like to feel that there is no past or future but to not care either way.

Creative people learn to savor whatever befalls them. Sometimes we wallow in wonder, sometimes we wallow in sorrow or confusion. But we learn to notice the finer details, even while those details wound or confound us.

When you approach experience in this way, you do become less of a victim and more of a creator. You gain some power when you choose to partake of any experience more wholeheartedly. You are not merely a person to whom things happen; you are a person who takes hold of whatever happens. That's a huge difference.

Don't be afraid to exploit your experience to the fullest. Don't back away from taking notes anytime and anywhere. Don't mind how people look at you when you talk about studying your depression. You've given up expecting people to understand how you operate anyway. It's a great day when you decide that no experience will be wasted on you.

What I've talked about in this chapter has more to do about owning your life than about being creative. But in order to be creative, you must own your life—all of it, even the parts you'd rather not have.

Though many books are published every year, not many are written from the wealth of resources a person taps when she faces her origins, her history, her personality and her experiences. So many deep, rich stories (or songs or paintings or sculptures) are waiting to be pulled up and shaped into understandable wisdom. So much history lies undisturbed when it could provide textured detail. So much healing waits for its time while creative people avoid their pain—in an effort, ironically, to do their work.

Spend real time mulling over your family and place. What aspect of your life have you not yet tapped? What regional proverb needs to be shaped for an audience? What history is lacking from your psychology? What ancient fear or desire is missing from your own motivation, or from the motivation of some character in poem or song?

✑ Exercises for a Writer's Formation

Your Place

Sketch out—through words or images—the place that is now yours. Do you live in an apartment, in a house, in a subdivision, in an old building, in a definable neighborhood, far from any neighbors? What are the main forms of transportation where you live? What are the ebbs and flows of a typical weekday there? Who are your neighbors? What institutions are nearby? What businesses?

Your People

Describe the people in your life as though they were characters in a play. Describe them physically and emotionally. Describe their likes and dislikes, their habits, their gifts. What is heroic about them, pathetic about them?

Your Time

Write an essay that distinguishes this decade from the decade directly before it. Use as many physical senses as you can.

Who Are You?

You are standing outside yourself and introducing yourself to a total stranger. Use no more than one hundred words.

Your Experiences

Pick five incidents from your life and turn them into little stories. Give each a beginning, a middle and an end. Do your best to include conflict, struggle, surprise, climax and resolution.

Instead of burying any more artists and writers, let's bury the myth that booze is a muse, that alcohol and drugs are a spur to creativity. The path to creativity begins with clarity, which means clearing the mind and body of substances that numb the senses and cloud perception.

DAN WAKEFIELD, *RELEASING THE CREATIVE SPIRIT*

We can only say that in exhibitionist, escapist forms of creativity there is no real encounter, no engagement with reality.

ROLLO MAY, *THE COURAGE TO CREATE*

This painful cycle—threatening thought, anxious reaction, and full retreat—is a fundamental cycle in the lives of creative people. Most creators are not aware of the existence of this cycle or that anxiety is a mighty brake preventing them from creating. . . . Most creators do not give anxiety its due.

ERIC MAISEL, *THE VAN GOGH BLUES*

The healthier I am, the more likely it is that I'll experience depression simply because I find it so hard to reach my lofty goals.

ERIC MAISEL, *THE VAN GOGH BLUES*

Although it is possible to be creative without having experienced personal trauma, such experiences often jolt people into asking questions that other people have no reason to ask and gaining a new perspective on realities that other people take for granted.

ROBERT WUTHNOW, *CREATIVE SPIRITUALITY*

8 THE BEAUTY AND DANGER OF A CREATIVE LIFE

Why the Wonder Brings Darkness with It

With the benefit of hindsight, I calculate that my first real depression occurred in February of 1984. I was in my mid-twenties and living in Jordan, teaching school as part of a two-year program that was a Southern Baptist version of the Peace Corps. I loved the country, the people and the work, and I still believe that the two years spent in the "hills of Gilead" were possibly the best two of my life. But by February I'd been in the country about six months, and winter in Ajloun, a village in the northwest region, begins in early autumn and ends in late spring. The temperature rarely dips to freezing, but the constant damp chills you to the bone. Between the frequent rain and the ever-present mountain fog, you might go days and days without seeing the sun.

Moreover, my heart was broken. During Christmas break I'd fallen for a Canadian diving instructor in the Gulf of Aqaba, and I'd been foolish enough to return there for my birthday in January, in hopes of getting him to fall for me. It was a horrible failure, and that deep disappointment set in motion a cycle that I was unable to break for nearly two months. I would have crying spells two or three times a day. I wasn't interested in anything, just tried to drag myself from a day of teaching to bedtime. Absolutely nothing brought comfort. The sadness went much deeper than what the romantic longings merited, and I sensed even then that I was dealing with something large and constant that underlay my temporary struggles. I gradually pulled out of this, with much prayer and moaning. Delayed culture shock probably figured into my state, but at that time all I knew was that I must manage another year and a half in this situation and be a grownup about it. I would teach songs and the English alphabet to my lovely Arab kindergarteners and first-graders and put to rest any other dreams.

Two years later, when I was teaching in the Missouri public school system, I spun into another period of bleak nothing, also during winter, but it was triggered primarily by loads of stress. I was barely making enough money to live on, and my father was struggling mightily with diabetes, which he'd had for several years but had up till then been able to regulate. I felt death at the door. And I was stuck in a small town with hardly any single people my age, more sure than ever that I would remain the family spinster.

After two years in Missouri, I returned to Jordan for a year as auxiliary staff, this time working primarily with church musicians. I'd decided to return to the place I loved while I applied to grad school, with the hope of making a transition from teaching to something else. The constant immersion in students didn't suit my introversion, and I was developing nodules on the vocal cords—I couldn't possibly do twenty-some more years of this work until retirement. Again in February I took a dive, and it was most directly related to some dynamics of the organization I worked for, but I suspected that ever since the broken heart in Aqaba, I was cycling around to depression about every February. That blackness did not lift for nearly a month.

The next year I was in grad school, exactly where I knew I should be. I was getting a master's in print communication—finally a closer connection to writing—but I started in the January term, in frigid, windblown Chicago. I was broke, alone and in an unfamiliar city, and by late February I was taking two or three showers a day just to help me gear up for the next task. The constant emotional pain—which felt quite physical—lifted only when I was writing; fortunately my courses provided lots of writing assignments with deadlines. This time the depression was severe enough that my thoughts turned regularly to knives and what a relief it would be to feel blade upon wrist. At a rational level I knew that this really wasn't what I wanted, but I did get scared and went to the student health center. I ended up on an antidepressant, which didn't help much and which I could not possibly afford, but by the time I figured all that out the depression had lifted pretty much on its own.

The next black spell came a few years later; it lasted longer but was not so severe, and fortunately I'd found a therapist who was good for me. By then my father was dead and I had passed the forty-year mark, walking into full-blown midlife crisis. I had also lost my only pregnancy, had left a faith community badly wounded, and had finally faced the reality of my husband's more severe and chronic depression, which did, and probably always would, require a complicated cocktail to keep him stable.

Although these depressive periods have generally happened in winter, I really enjoy winter weather—the snow, the grayness, the bundling up and walking through bare woods, all the marvelous hot soups and drinks. Autumn is absolutely the best time for my creativity, and my writing usually flies through the winter months. But every year I approach January and February with care. I suspect that the cycle has more to do with emotional history than with physiology. Regardless of the cause, it is part of my life.

If my creative gifts had any effect on the depressions, it was to provide healing. As long as I stayed engaged in writing or singing, I maintained enough equilibrium to keep going. But I believe that the sensitive personality that is able to reach deep down and gather the right images and memories is the same sensitive personality that is easily wounded by the normal hurts and disappointments of the world. I always cried easily and tired quickly, depressed or not. And still I wear out in record time, especially when I'm writing. Most of the time it's a healthy form of worn-out, but long ago I had to accept my limitations when it comes to energy. I go in surges, and I've learned how to work with that.

THE DARKNESS THAT ACCOMPANIES REVELATION

When you're dealing with something as soulful as your creativity, it's good to develop some healthy respect for its inherent power. It's equally important to acknowledge the transcendent character of creativity as well as its tendency to stir up all of life. Creativity emerges from the human soul, and this is a complex entity. Your creative vision resides there—and so do your fears. Your beliefs reside there—and so do your prejudices. It's no simple thing to go to your soul and work with what you find there.

It's helpful to remember that there's a shadow side to your gifts. Truth always has a cutting edge. Every revelation brings some darkness with it. It's important that you learn how that darkness affects you.

Nothing is more dazzling than creative discovery: the paragraph in the story that seems to fall right out of heaven onto the page; the accident of color or texture that opens up the canvas; the solution that no one was even looking for. And nothing can be more dark and frightening than what the soul discovers when yet another layer of the self is pulled back. The peeling of layers is what happens as we grow in our creative gifts.

DO ARTISTS HAVE TO SUFFER IN ORDER TO PRODUCE GOOD ART?

Our culture has tended to accept certain images of the artistic personality. We think of artists as somewhat unstable. They go through relationships and day jobs like crazy. They are intensely your best friend one day and hardly know you exist the next. They neglect their family. They drink too much. They keep unhealthy schedules. And so on. We rather enjoy, from a distance, the pathos and chaos of the stereotypical artist's life.

We've allowed a few flamboyant artistic folks to paint this picture for us, and we've ignored the many productive people in the creative arts who are stable in their relationships and who, except for their wonderful art, live fairly mundane lives. But the stereotype exists because many artistic people do struggle.

Imagine a seventeen-year-old painter. He has tapped into his gifts early, and he's full of vision and vitality. His creativity takes him straight to his soul, because that's where creativity happens. What does this young man find there? He finds fears, sins and wounds that many people never face until they're twenty-five or thirty. He has dived right into his gifts, unaware of what else will be waiting in that soul place. So not only is he producing art that has his high school teacher weeping, he is fighting spiritual battles he never expected to face. These are battles that he is likely unprepared to face: his culture, even his religious culture, has not acknowledged these needs and thus has not helped him prepare to meet them.

Imagine a fourteen-year-old girl who has been abused her whole life. Through a music teacher at school, she discovers that she can sing. She begins to sing, and there is a depth and wonder to her voice and her approach that astound those who hear her. What they don't understand is that this poor child has had to get acquainted with her soul just to survive living in her parents' home. She has been fighting hard battles for years. As she dwelt in that interior place, she bumped into creative gifts she never dreamed she had.

So which comes first, the suffering or the art? Doesn't matter. What these two stories have in common is that in each case the person connected with his or her creative gifts along with darkness and struggle. If you are creative early in life, you will meet your "shadow" sooner.

If you suffer early in life, and if creative opportunities open up to you, such as high school choir, you are quite likely to get acquainted with your creativity.

What do we do with this? For the seventeen-year-old artist, we find someone to help his spirit, because whether he's in a spiritual mood or not, he is dealing with spiritual things, and he's going to need support. For the fourteen-year-old girl, we provide spiritual help too, because her gifts will take her only so far toward healing. Her songs won't solve everything. But in nurturing her songs we have found a handle by which to take hold of her healing.

Absent too much of the time is an understanding of how closely related the spiritual is to the creative. Also absent is the understanding that people need spiritual help when they are learning their creativity. What they need is *creative formation,* an intentional working with their creative gifts so that the whole person is nurtured. This need for creative formation is what has driven the writing of this book; indeed, it has led me to become a facilitator of workshops that deal with the intersections between creativity and spirituality.

I believe that if we learned how to provide spiritual direction in the context of creative gifts, far fewer artists would be overwhelmed by depression and panic, and many more people would discover and develop their gifts. As it is now, some people who are brave enough and compelled enough to explore their creativity get into trouble but don't have the help they need. Others who are spiritually centered enough to understand what their gifts might stir up don't develop their gifts because they are afraid of facing the shadows.

When we allow God to cradle us as we grow, we can become the creative people we were meant to be. We can follow our gifts to the center of our soul, and we can face the difficult things that wait for us there. We can navigate the darkness, and we can nourish our gifts. But none of this just happens as a matter of course. We won't be safe and sure if we don't respect what we are doing and how risky that work can be.

⚬ COMMON SOURCES OF DARKNESS

There are numerous ways in which the artist encounters turmoil and darkness. Much of our conflict and pain is just like anyone else's, but certain aspects of the artist's life make it ripe for soul disturbance.

Isolation

Much artistic work is done in solitude. It often requires that a person devise strategies and make major decisions on his own. The novelist, not his wife or writing coach, must decide whether the protagonist lives or dies at the end of the story. The painter has to determine the direction of her next set of pieces. The sculptor and no one else looks at a work in progress and either finishes it or starts over again. Whereas many other decisions and plans are made along with significant others, you face that tension alone when it comes to your work. Don't underestimate how much this may drain you.

Not only that, but the sheer number of hours you may need to spend entirely alone can make you feel as if when you join your family for dinner you are emerging from a deep cave. Suddenly you must come into the light and talk to people, hang out, laugh at jokes, watch a movie, help make a salad or set the table. The shift can feel huge, depending on how deeply you have been absorbed in your work.

What you have to do is define good and bad isolation and get the company you need. Ask yourself some simple questions.

- When does isolation help my work?
- When does isolation feel painful or full of anxiety?
- Who is good company for me—who makes my heart lighter and my outlook brighter?
- Who is good for my development—who challenges me in the right ways and helps me stick with my work?
- How often do I need to be with people? What do I need from them?

After you've worked with these questions, make some choices. Set aside time to be alone with your work; honor that time and do not apologize for it or entertain guilt about it. When isolation seems detrimental, give yourself permission to take yourself out of isolation. This means that you won't worry about the creative work you have temporarily left. It will be there when you return.

Make a point to spend time with people who are good for you and good for your work. It may be a weekly coffee break or an afternoon walk every few weeks. Or you and a friend might check in with each other before beginning work. One friend of mine does this almost daily—just a quick e-mail before his writing time. Come up with some way of giving yourself good company at the right times.

At the risk of stating the obvious: A Christian needs regular worship and fellowship during times of intense creative activity just as at any other time. You may need it more then, even if the work makes you feel like hiding.

Rejection

Creative works beg responses from others. When you complete a work and announce that it's finished, you must deal with how people react to it. If your work has truly issued from the well, bringing all sorts of power with it, you are likely to stir up both negative and positive responses. Some folks just won't get what you're doing. Others will think they understand while it's clear to you that they are oversimplifying or forming their own conclusions. If your work is made public, as in the publishing of a novel, then you must deal with whatever the reviewers say, or with the possibility that no one will say anything.

Sooner or later the artist faces criticism if not outright rejection. Rejection never feels good, even if at a rational level you're not that concerned about it. When others witness your creativity and don't respect it or appreciate it, you feel pain.

One way to deal with rejection is to stand back periodically and view your work as being on a continuum. It will never be perfect, but it will be on a course of development throughout your life. Each work is valuable and praiseworthy because it fits a certain time and phase for you. An early novel will likely not be as well crafted as a later one, but you wouldn't get to the better-crafted novel if you hadn't written the lesser one first. The reader who rejects a work is rejecting one work at one time; that's all.

You have to take into account who is rejecting you and why. Does this reviewer not like your work because of its flaws or because the reviewer is biased against its genre or the viewpoint it presents? Does the person who rejects your work have any real credentials for judging it? If you were to have coffee with the person who has disparaged your painting or story, would the conversation move you to want his friendship, or would it confirm that you have little in common with him anyway? You won't always be able to answer these questions, but it helps to remember that everybody will not like you all the time; it stands to reason that everybody won't like your every creative endeavor.

Ultimately you have to grow a tough skin so that rejection simply won't matter that much. Accept that some people will not get what you're doing. You don't create art for them; you create it for those it helps and enlightens. Let go of everyone else.

Energy Depletion

As a creative, you are out at the edges of experience and understanding. You are in a near constant state of exploration, with senses heightened on a regular basis. All of this takes enormous amounts of energy. Think of how tired you were after your first session of doing anything—learning to use a pottery wheel, doing dramatic improvisation, using a new software system, learning to play tennis. You went home exhausted, because it was new and you were trying to absorb it. You were much more tired that first time than you were after subsequent sessions.

When you are getting to know a new character, that's a new experience. When you sit for an hour finding alternative words, phrases or scenes, that's exploration. Creative work takes loads of energy. Many artists have a surge existence—working like mad for a period and then crashing in order to recover from all that work. Many of us don't make good nine-to-five employees because our natural energies go up and down to accommodate our gifts. Even as a book editor I surge. When I'm in a surge, I can get a lot of work done in a short time—and it's good work. But if I'm not in a surge, just checking grammar feels like walking through hip-deep water. Early in my publishing career I figured out how to work with this type of energy without endangering my job. When editing felt too laborious or unproductive, I would shift to one of many other tasks that were part of my job. I've found that midafternoon is a good time to answer correspondence or catch up on professional reading, because the editing synapses are simply not firing too well for me at that time of day.

About two years ago I cut back to editing part time so that I could give more time to my writing. I made the step with some trepidation, because anyone who works in publishing knows how few writers support themselves by writing alone. But my publisher agreed to keep me on part time. I would come to the office two to three days per week; the other days I would be writing at home.

I foolishly assumed that "writing at home" would translate into eight- or at least six-hour days. For a couple of months I struggled to maintain that kind of writing time but never did. So I started querying other writers and was relieved to find that many of them considered four hours of writing a full workday. The remaining hours of the day often fill up with writing-related activities, but four solid hours of putting words together is considered by many artists to be a good day's work.

This was hard to accept, because I'd spent years putting in the typical corporate work week. Now I'm learning to relax and find the best ways to use my time. I really can write only a few hours on a given day, although when I occasionally go away for a two- or three-day writing retreat I often clock six hours per day; it is easier when I'm not responsible for household tasks, checking e-mail or answering the phone. I have had to readjust the way I see work, specifically the way I see *my* work. Once energy is spent, it must be replenished—simple as that. I can push to write another hour or two, and sometimes I do, but overall I function best by giving my most refreshed self to the work for fewer hours.

Accept that the healthy creative life takes a lot of energy and that you will need to rest. Accept that your workday will not look like the workday of many other people. Just expect to get tired, because you are working hard. Get tired, rest and then work some more.

Anxiety

According to Eric Maisel, therapist and author of *The Van Gogh Blues*, most artists grossly underestimate how greatly they are affected by anxiety. The emotions you experience upon merely looking at a blank page or canvas can send you running to find to all sorts of distractions (Maisel theorizes that the anxiety of facing the blank whatever is what fuels the addictive behavior common among artists). For many of us, anxiety leads right into fatigue and then depression.

Anxiety is an important component of creativity because it provides tension and energy and sharpens your senses. Just as you should welcome healthy fear, welcome healthy anxiety. When you feel the anxiety moving in, ask yourself why you're worried or scared.

There is always some anxiety floating in the atmosphere once I'm under contract for a book. I want this book to be flawless. I want it to garner exceptional reviews and make lots of money for the publisher and for me. The anxiety keeps me edgy enough to push always toward my best. This is not anxiety that I want to lose for the sake of feeling a little calmer.

But some anxiety is an indication that some unfinished business or an unnamed fear is lurking. Figure it out. Write in your journal. Talk to a friend. Line out exactly what's making your heart race. Often the simple naming of it will decrease its power almost immediately.

Recently I felt paralyzed and couldn't get myself to work on any of my writing projects. About midmorning I wrote down in my journal

everything that was going on that day that didn't feel good. When I
finished listing everything, I was amazed that I could function at all:
the day was filled with appointments, problem solving and inner conflicts that needed to be dealt with. I really should have felt worse than
I did! Next I wrote out how I planned to deal with each thing, and
then I was able to start moving again. I had named my anxiety and
given myself little steps to take. Sounds simple, but we often miss the
simple solutions.

Artistic anxiety can be dealt with just as you deal with any other
anxiety. If you utter the Jesus Prayer (some version of "Lord have
mercy, Christ have mercy") when you are anxious in general, it will
probably be effective in those moments when the blank page feels
overwhelming.

Expect to be anxious. Be grateful for healthy anxiety that keeps
your work going and keeps you alert. Learn how to talk to yourself
when the anxiety comes.

Exploration

When your creative work pushes boundaries and reworks standard
definitions, you encounter tension and discomfort. Sometimes you
just want to do something cliché and boring rather than enter such
discomfort. Sometimes you'd rather not have to think and struggle.

Play with exploration and learn to shift in and out of it. Creativity
is not only exploration. Your creative work involves many components, and when exploration makes you weary, try doing something
else for a while. I will free-write a character for only so long and then
drop him or her and do something left-brained and nonexploratory.
This is one of the beauties of the creative process; it contains ebb and
flow and allows for shifts between tasks. It's really all right for you to
take up a simple writing assignment that won't require much more
than putting ideas together. Your every creative task does not need to
delve into the depths or break new ground. Try giving yourself easy
assignments sometimes—to write in a particular poetry form for an

afternoon or make up a page of formula plots. Those things feed your gifts too, and in the process you give yourself a little break.

Occupational Wear and Tear

It does seem that artistic temperaments are more prone to depression than are other temperaments. I suspect that this is because depression often manifests in facets of the personality an artist works with all the time: emotion, passion and intuition. Is it possible that we manifest our ailments of soul in ways that are most likely to speak to us? If you're not the contemplative type, a pain in the lower back will get your attention faster than will a series of disturbing dreams. If you spend your days working with words and roaming your own head and heart, then a break in the flow of creativity will alert you to trouble sooner than an upset stomach will. Why wouldn't the soul use whatever is most effective?

I have learned that my soul alerts me through fatigue, and I'm sure this is because I'm an on-task sort of person. Even though I have an artistic temperament, I'm a list keeper and very achievement oriented. Being forced to slow down my activity bothers me a lot. When I go through several days of being unable to even make a list, I know I'm in trouble. I may get aches and pains, but for me those are easier to ignore than an interrupted schedule, whether that's a schedule for housecleaning or for creative writing.

What causes athletes most of their suffering? The very joints and muscles that they use constantly. Many professional athletes reach their middle years with physical limitations that are direct results of their very physical early career. In the same way, people who do soul work—creative work—as their "job" are spending much more time with those facets of the human personality that fall victim to depression and similar disturbances. It should be no surprise that people who work constantly in the realm of emotions, ideas and intuitions also pay a price in those areas of their life. Your soul work will take a toll on your interior life, just as the athlete's work takes a toll on joints and muscles.

Don't be shocked when your work wears on your soul. Take that as an indication that you are in fact working hard and that probably something good will come of it. Then do whatever you need to do to care for yourself. Take time off, go play, soak in whatever feeds your inner self—an hour at the spa or gym, a stroll through a favorite park or gallery, a feel-good novel or movie, a retreat with books, prayers and quiet.

Increased Sensitivity

An artist has to become super-sensitive to life in order to notice what others miss and to develop what others may ignore or consider unimportant. The longer you work at your creative gifts, the more sensitive you become.

Of course this means that you're more sensitive to *everything*. Not only can you identify multiple textures in that stone wall, but you can identify multiple conflicts in the life of a friend. You notice sadness or anger in the eyes of passing strangers. Increased sensitivity will nourish your art, but it will wear on you at times. You may cry more easily or be more prone to obsess over some horrible event in the news.

Be grateful that you cry easily or that you pick up readily on people's motives. This means that your senses are fine-tuned, and that's good for your art.

I am able to watch disturbing films—in fact I try to watch a wide range of films, because it helps me write better dialogue and it awakens my visual senses. But certain things invariably upset me, and so there are some films I will never go to see. I know that I can bear about one war film per year, and I never watch it a second time. I saw *Platoon* and *The Killing Fields* because I thought they were important for me to see as an American citizen. I saw *Schindler's List* for the same reason. But I waited until they came out on video, and I watched them (separately, of course) at home with just my husband, during times when I wasn't embroiled in emotional struggles. I hope that I am always deeply upset at the viciousness of war. I will probably never see a film about organized crime because I'm ultra-sensitive to cruelty and torture. I won't apologize for this sensitivity; I believe my sensitivity to such things will enable me to write about them in a way that makes clear to readers how awful they are. I won't need a page of gore to describe some violent scene; I'll simply choose a sentence or two that makes the horror clear enough—and that makes the reader feel it acutely.

Pay attention to the things that really disturb or bother you. You can allow appropriate recovery time if you know that hearing a particular symphony will move you so much that you'll need to walk and weep for an hour afterward.

And you'll have to dismiss what others may say about how sensitive you are. They may chuckle or sigh at how easily you are affected by things. They'll probably tell you to grow a tougher skin or to not take things so personally. Well, they aren't writing this screenplay or creating this art therapy program for homeless women. You are doing good work, and sensitivity is a requirement. If you grow a tough skin, it should be the one that repels the sighs and remarks of people who don't live in your world or do your work.

Narcissism

Less developed artists especially struggle with this. The fact is, you have to be somewhat in love with yourself and your gifts if you are to have the gall to write a story and expect others to read it. Self-absorption is at times a given. And if you spend most of your time thinking about yourself, expect to get depressed.

Just yesterday I was out walking because I was too tired to do anything more useful. I'd spent the week working on the revision of this manuscript, and part of that revision—requested by editor and reviewers—was that I include more of my own story. A week of digging back into my own stuff was pretty tiring. So I was trying to refuel by walking to nowhere in particular.

Suddenly I said to myself, *You know, I've been me for forty-six years, and I'm ready to be someone else now. How can we manage that?* I will be so relieved to finish this work and get back to my fiction. Focus on the self takes you to your own limits and eventually highlights what you don't like about yourself.

There are a couple of answers to the narcissism that comes so naturally to the artist. It helps a lot to view yourself in the larger spectrum of artists and to submit yourself very intentionally to that higher creative process. Madeleine L'Engle has spoken and written about being in service to the work. A service mentality can bring balance to the narcissism.

And forgive me for repeating myself, but healthy community will drag you back from the brink of total self-absorption. Welcome people into your life, even a few who challenge and irritate you. Acquire your artistic partners, mentors, critics, supporters. Even more important, lend your support to others in their creative work.

With each new book contract I'm offered, at least one of my colleagues will ask when I'm going to quit the editing job and write full time. But I see this writing life as giving as well as receiving, and when I serve other writers in the capacity of editor, I am giving. When I write, I'm receiving the art that's waiting for me. When I present workshops I'm giving (and by the way, I'm rarely able to do any writing, even in downtime, when I'm in workshop mode), and I'm receiving too, from the gifts of other writers. It's a large cycle, a circle of community, and I don't want to break it. Whatever course my dual career takes, I hope that I'll always be able to balance the giving and receiving. I think this is the way it's supposed to be. I am glad that on a regular basis I must take the focus off myself entirely in order to help another person develop his or her gifts.

Dried-Up Well

I don't believe that anyone's well is ever really dry, but sometimes it seems that way. There's not an idea left in your head. You have no vigor for what usually is a pleasure. Your blank stare out the window really is that—blank—rather than contemplation that takes you to a place of inspiration. Your own work bores you. You try to tap the well, and all you get is a belch or two.

My writing life has been very busy for months now, and because I don't expect this to always be the case, I've thrown myself into the multiple projects and simply accepted that I have months to go before I can rest much. There are days when I fear that my bucket will come up empty, with just some shriveled dead flies and spiders in the bottom. Early in the summer I really worried about this. I had six book projects in the works in one form or another, and I kept having ominous visions of burning out in late June and having to send back all my advance money.

One frustration was that I couldn't afford much time to write in my journal. I've never written daily in any journal—I just don't operate that way. But I'd gone days and days without journaling, and that didn't seem healthy.

I'd been hearing for years that writers should read poetry on a regular basis. But because my writing gifts have never manifested much in poetry and I really don't "get" a lot of literary poetry, I had shied away from reading it. A good friend of mine is a poet, and she suggested a couple of anthologies that would be accessible to people like me who are somewhat afraid of real poetry. I bought three different books and began reading two or three poems every morning.

This was quite enjoyable, and it occurred to me that maybe I should resume journaling, only in poetry form. Maybe if I didn't have to write pages of long lines of prose, I could get back to my journals. If I journaled through poetry, I would have to focus more quickly, down to the real issue, and choose my words more carefully; I pictured this as easier and less time consuming than page after page of meandering conversation with myself to figure out what I was feeling.

So I went to a bookstore and found a small journal with unlined pages. It was so narrow that I couldn't write long lines of any kind. Good, I would be forced to journal in short form.

It is now September; the journal is nearly full, and it is all poetry, quite focused and just as powerful as any of my former long pages have been. A new little underground spring has been uncovered, and I just might journal this way for a long time.

During the winter I will likely fill up my well by visiting museums and art galleries, drinking in color and form while the outdoors become more muted and uninviting. It's likely that I will have to go on the hunt for new sources from time to time, because every well has its low seasons.

You have to figure out what fills you up—what activities prime your pump. As an artist you will give, give, give of your inner resources. So you must also take in on a regular basis. What refreshes you? What inspires you? What gives you energy for your work? Make it a point to fill up regularly. Be sure to witness—and to do—things that fill you with wonder.

Natural Stages of Dormancy

Most people go through cycles. In just about every cycle there's a period of dormancy, when it seems that nothing much is happening. Sometimes this is when you think your well has dried up. You can't imagine having another good idea ever again. You're not interested in your work. Creativity doesn't mean as much, or if it means anything, you can't really connect with it.

You may need to rest and get away from your work for a while. Most artists need regular breaks, even if they don't come often or last long. Try to step back and see what stages you've gone through before. You may be able to identify a stage of inactivity and then label it "dormant time" and stop worrying about it.

The Bad That Comes with the Good

Creative work takes you to that interior place where all your "stuff" is. You can't deal with the unconscious world without awakening the disturbing dreams, memories, struggles and grief that are there along with the wondrous things. I've written three novels, and each in its own way hooked into my very personal life. I couldn't explore relationships between the characters without dealing with my own relationships. I had to imagine some things that were not part of my personal experience, such as getting caught up in an adulterous relationship or what it would feel like to put the barrel of a pistol in my mouth. Heavy stuff. And if you tap into it enough to write in a passionate, compelling way, you pay an emotional price. It's part of your work.

I believe that our creative gifts are given to us for many reasons. One purpose is our own healing. When your creative work brings you face to face with your personal demons, find whatever help you need. Years ago I began seeing a therapist because I was badly depressed and in over my head. I still see that therapist from time to time, because he helps me interpret the stuff I encounter in the course of my writing life. Not every artist needs a therapist, but every artist does need some way of dealing with the bad stuff that emerges in the creative process. You may work well with journaling or reading books or hashing through issues with one or two good friends. You may find healing through spiritual disciplines or seeing a pastoral counselor or spiritual director. The important thing is to find what you need.

✑ SEXUAL POWER IN THE LIFE OF ART

Because artists are naturally tuned in to the world through their senses, it only follows that they have been stereotyped as bohemian people who readily get sexually involved with others. This is a gross generalization, but I do think that most artists are highly sensitive to the physical, and therefore sexual, world.

We may get into bed for all the right reasons and discover only later that there's more to it than that. If creative types are often tempted to sexual intimacy, it's not because they are immoral people; it's because they are in love with life and open to a variety of experiences. The passion that fuels creativity is akin to the passion that fuels sexuality.

Spiritual guidance can spare us a lot of pain here. It's important that we understand what our sexual boundaries are and why. It's not enough to merely accept the moral rules passed on to us by earlier times or a religious system. It's also not enough to simply accept the boundaries—or lack of boundaries—imposed by whatever mood is prevailing in the present culture. We must explore—through our spirituality and our creative gifts—what it really means to have sexual integrity and freedom.

It's not that a person makes her own rules; it's that sooner or later she must understand at a deep level why any rules are worthy to be followed. When we're children, sometimes we have to accept as a parent's explanation, "Because I say so," and that authority is enough. As adults, it is our task to mature, to understand the reasons for boundaries and integrate them into the way we think and operate. Because the topic of sexuality is volatile, we have tended to simply rely on—or ignore—the boundaries without thoughtfully integrating their rationale. We tend either to hand over all responsibility to authority or to rebel against authority. A thoughtful life cannot progress this way.

Creative surges can become sexual surges. How and why is this so? Well, when your creative juices are flowing, a lot of things start to happen in you.

You Become Highly Interested in Life

It can be the most mundane hour and the most uninspiring weather. The people you see are the people who are usually around you. But all of this brightens up and becomes focused in ways that are not usual. Your neighbor bending over a stubborn lawn chair becomes a little poem. The whine of the tired three-year-old becomes a bit of description in the scene you're writing. That person who always seemed boring and unattractive appears now to be a person with a whole history you'd like to know. You wake up.

You Get Impatient with Negativity

There are just too many important things to think about right now for you to be griping or in a funk. The irritations that usually make you cranky are hardly on your radar today. Something inside you has re-arranged your priorities, because it knows that you have very cool work to do.

You're Not Self-Conscious

It's impossible to be in the flow of work and be self-conscious at the same time. You're either worried about yourself or focused on your work; you can't be both. When you're in the midst of creative work, you're probably more at home with yourself than at any other time. You move naturally rather than awkwardly.

You Fall in Love with Yourself for a Change

There are degrees of this. Depending on how much you loathe or love yourself usually, this aspect of creativity may or may not be a key dynamic. But you're ignoring negative things more. Also the critical person in you is a little scared of alienating the person in you who is creating, so you are naturally kinder to yourself during a creative surge. Your soul cannot afford to be at war with itself.

You Have a Terrific Ability to Focus

Your soul is homing in on something grand, even if that grand thing is merely a terrible first draft. Your soul understands how important it is to concentrate. Unless you are really fatigued or ill, this is one time when concentration is not a problem.

I'm sure there are other things that happen to you during a time of creativity. But let's sum up for now and see what kind of person you've become:

- You are interested in everything, and therefore you yourself are interesting.
- You are positive rather than negative.
- You seem to be happy and at home with yourself.
- You are focused.
- Your whole self is open and receptive to the world.

What happens to people around you when you get like this?

The people who live with you sort of stay out of your way. They like you this way, but you are not exactly manageable. They enjoy how much you are enjoying them and life in general, and they're glad that you're not noticing their bad points so much and not harping on problems. At the same time you're not willing to listen to *them* harp, and you're so focused on what you're doing that they feel a tad neglected. They wonder: if they died today, would you notice?

The people who don't live with you may well be awestruck. They had thought you were just that introverted writer next door, but lately you have a glow and you've gone out of your way to say hello. What's up? Coworkers notice how beautiful or handsome you are today, not because you've stepped up the clothes and makeup (although in this state maybe you have) but because you are more comfortable with yourself and more interested in life. A colleague asks you out to lunch. Some guy you hardly know flirts with you.

Herein lies a problem. There's a reason that during a creative season some people fall into intense relationships. A person who is really engaged with her creativity is a person whose soul is humming. You become more attractive at such times, even if you're forgetting to shower and you're short on sleep. Your deepest self is shining out of you, and other people will notice. Friends and family will notice. People will notice you in a sexual way too. With all the good that happens during a creative time, there's some danger to consider.

Perhaps it is this seductive quality of creativity that accounts for many romances in the workplace. When you are working at a heightened level of sensitivity, and you are working closely with another person who is also at that level, your souls are communing in an intimate way.

Does this mean that you are asking for a sexually promiscuous life if you say yes to your creative gifts? Not if you understand what dynamics are at work. For people who have ordered their life by a religious faith or a moral system, it is important to face these matters head on. You look at a situation, assess the danger and set up ways to protect yourself. You don't want to break up families or compel yourself or anyone else to break promises, to injure loved ones or to fragment anyone's life. So you do whatever you have to do. You set up the necessary boundaries.

And if you happen to fall in love, you remember that you are merely seeing in this person what is there all the time, what God sees constantly. It is wonderful that for a change you see it too, but that doesn't mean suddenly you have to rearrange your life.

New parents fall in love with their infant. A guy who is usually a hard driver at work, all business and results-oriented, suddenly becomes dreamy and distracted; he can't get his new little child out of his mind. He misses his baby and can't wait to get home to look at her some more. This is being in love.

I'm in love with my dog. We got her from the shelter when she was a year old, and she has some doggie issues that go with having been abused before we got her. But I look forward to seeing her when I come home. I know every mood of her expressive ears, and I enjoy the way she drapes herself dramatically across furniture when she wants attention. I love to stroke her soft face and belly, take her for walks and teach her tricks. I'm infatuated with this puppy; I am tuned in to her and appreciate every aspect of her furry little being.

The young father is not sexually attracted to his new baby, and I am not sexually attracted to my dog. But we are both madly in love. Falling in love is being overwhelmed by awareness of someone or something else. When you first discover a musician or actor or writer who really moves you, when you search out every CD or movie or book this person has ever contributed to, that's a form of being in love. It is extreme attentiveness. We have been conditioned to think of it in terms of sex, but that oversimplifies both attentiveness and sex.

We will likely fall in love many times, because it is in our nature to appreciate the wonder of other people. We will come awake again and again, which is a good thing. And we can survive those infatuations—

whether or not there's any sexual feeling involved—as long as we appreciate infatuation for what it really is.

So if you have been moved to take special notice of someone or something, take advantage of this season of heightened interest. Use it for your work, or simply allow yourself to get charged up by the intense feelings. But don't mistake it for a love affair that is destined to happen.

THE WARNING SIGNAL OF DEPRESSION

I suspect that there is such a thing as healthy depression. It's possible that the soul shuts down the person when the person doesn't have sense enough to shut herself down. And shut down we must from time to time, for simple rest, maintenance and repair. I go back to the mantra: Your soul knows more than the conscious you knows. You may have needed rest for weeks, but you're so ambitious or so brimming over with obligation that you have ignored your own signals. Or you've replaced true rest with something like a vacation for which you must spend a lot of money, endure airline travel and find your way through a strange environment. When your soul wants rest, it wants a cessation of activity on several levels. When you don't cease on your own, your soul is likely to cease you.

This is not a trapped-in-hopelessness, suicidal malaise. When you have become self-destructive or dangerous to others, your depression is not manageable and probably has its roots in something besides the need for soul rest. If you are dangerously depressed, seek professional help. I am well acquainted with people who struggle with incapacitating depression, and I would never say to them, "Oh, you just need some rest. Try listening to your soul!"

If, however, you just can't get out of bed as early as usual, if you're not concentrating well, if you're not very interested in life, if your creativity seems to have receded to some dark, deep place you can't reach, then consider that your soul is talking to you. It may be saying any of the following:

- You are sleep deprived. You've been burning the candle at both ends for too long. Go to bed and stay there as long as possible.
- You need to stop and wait. There's something you need to understand, learn or spend time with, and you can't do that until you hold still for a while.
- It's time to eliminate some stress. You cannot continue to function at the level you have been. You are doing too much, or you're trying to do it too fast, or you're doing it under the wrong kind of pressure. Let go of everything for a few days until your head clears and you can evaluate what's wrong.
- You are avoiding something difficult or dark. You can't put off the truth forever. Drop everything now and deal with it.
- You need to take a break from this particular task. It has required a lot of energy and information, and you need to refuel. It will be waiting for you when you come back to it. But leave it for a time. It's using you up.

Severe Depression Merits Serious Attention

When you cannot function and you grow hopeless, even to the point of contemplating your own death, a good rest or a change of pace will not be enough to set things right. You need professional help right away. Such severe depression will often require medication, at least for the short term, because usually this level of imbalance has physiological components. Severe depression that requires medication may have more to do with heredity or physical factors than with your temperament or work.

Artists have real reservations when it comes to medications, and for good reason. Some medications dull the senses and short-circuit creativity. Most heavy-duty meds deliver side effects, and it's a personal call as to which life is better—the medicated, safe and dispassionate one or the more dangerous, vigorous and creative one. With the right doctors and enough experimentation, often a medium can be reached between these two extremes. And not only are we coming up with more medications, today's meds work more effectively and accurately than those from even a few years ago. There is hope.

It's a difficult journey, and I believe that a person who struggles with ongoing depression deserves the same empathy as someone who battles cancer. Because depression is related to emotional and mental instability, it has long been regarded as a character flaw or even a spiritual transgression. And often it has few physical symptoms that are obvious, so a deeply depressed person can appear to be okay.

If you suffer from depression, my heart goes out to you, because you won't receive much empathy, and you will be tempted to avoid getting the help you need. Your depression may be a condition that can be helped greatly by medication, therapy or a combination of the two. If it's mild depression, you can find practices that will help you, such as exercising, avoiding alcohol and other mood-altering substances, or meditating regularly. This may simply be the tough part of your existence, that thing that will always demand some attention. You may need to spend a significant chunk of money and time working with it and seeking to dwell productively with it.

I often wonder how much more creative certain artists would have been if they had learned how to care for their soul. If that writer could produce such marvelous works in the throes of clinical depression, what could she have done in a healthier state? How much better could that opium-addicted artist have painted if he had been free of addiction and its anxiety? People who are not developing their spirituality along with their creativity may feel that they *need* the depression or addiction in order to work. And society tends to enjoy the drama of their sad life stories. But I believe it is possible to care for your soul and be creative too. In fact when our soul is doing well, our creativity has more freedom to do what it is meant to do.

It's tempting to use creative work as a form of self-medication. While that's effective to a point—it helped me maintain equilibrium during grad school—creativity is designed to flourish, not merely help you survive. It will probably not flourish with any consistency when your soul is ill.

⚜ THE BALANCE THAT IS ILLUSION

Should you even expect to maintain balance if you throw yourself into the whirl of the creative life? Probably not. Balance is generally impossible. It is also overrated. The balance many of us crave and strive for is really an illusion.

The spiritual, creative life has its seasons, and like weather seasons they are often sloppy and unpredictable. Growth itself is sloppy and unpredictable; whoever suggested that any of this could be carried out in a calm and happy manner?

On one end of the spectrum are people who suffer unnecessary guilt over every inconsistency and missed appointment. Some of us get too hyper about doing the right things at the right times every day, never making mistakes and never forgetting important tasks. Such anxiety kills creativity, and it gives us ulcers and insomnia. We have to give up on doing everything right. Few, if any, people care whether I plan a healthy menu or keep up my three weekly sessions of exercise or answer that letter within a certain time frame. It's fine that I have goals, but the goals are merely tools, not the end itself.

Imbalance Results from Neglected Relationships

On the other end of the spectrum are people who feel that they are justified when in order to follow a creative calling they renege on crucial commitments. It's always necessary to balance work and relationships, but don't expect the balance to be easy. Some days you'll ignore your loved ones because your process is just chugging along and it would be too costly to bring it to a screeching stop. Well, some days your loved ones will ignore you too. We don't suffer great harm from occasional days of neglect. When we neglect one another consistently, though, and in effect relegate important relationships to a place of unimportance, this is imbalance that merits attention.

Back when I couldn't afford to cut back on editing in order to write, I spent a lot of weekends and vacation time writing. My husband was supportive, and fortunately he's an introvert too, so he didn't complain when I spent hours to myself, even when we were on what should have been leisure trips. It was only after the year of the second novel that he said he hoped I could cut back on my other work so I wouldn't have to write every spare minute.

I consider that I have two major callings right now. One is to be married to Jim, and the other is to write and to nurture other writers through the workshops I facilitate. Both of these callings make up who I am, and I cannot compromise either calling without compromising myself. I am, in part, the writer I am because I am married to Jim. I am, in part, the life partner I am because of how my gifts have developed me as a person. When one of those callings begins to be sacrificed for the other, it is time to stop and evaluate what I'm doing and how.

During those years of full-time work and writing on the side, even on vacations, I made a commitment to go to bed when Jim went to bed. Whether or not we had sex, bedtime was an important time of connection for us. We would talk, snuggle, relax, process the day and regroup. Sometimes I would go to bed for that time of fellowship and then get up and write another hour or so. But most of the time I got up earlier in the morning to write rather than miss bedtime with my husband.

Each person has to sort out for herself the level of commitment that's needed for her major callings. Every marriage has to hit its own stride, and every healthy marriage develops the flexibility that allows both partners to grow into the people they are gifted to become. I doubt that marriages end simply because a spouse decides to follow a calling. Those marriages were already in jeopardy to begin with; the flexibility was lacking when one or the other spouse began to grow. If it hadn't been a writing or acting career, something else would have brought on the crisis, because the relationship was too brittle to withstand healthy give-and-take.

Imbalance Results from Impulsive Shifts

We have to be careful not to follow our callings too haphazardly. Some people try to do too much too fast, making plans that soon overwhelm them. Or they assume that because one aspect of life is changing, every other aspect must get rearranged as well. In the midst of personal transition or crisis, they decide that the tension or discomfort comes from the husband or wife and so they must dispose of that relationship; they fail to deal with the real crisis, which is their own. Or they spend far too much money or dump the day job before they've even developed basic creative habits.

When a person flames out while trying to reach unrealistic goals, often her relationships flame out as well. But her problem is not that she tried to embrace a creative calling but that she tried to do so too impulsively. You make a lot of choices when you commit yourself to your creative gifts, and sometimes you make bad choices for the right reasons. This is why community is so important, why you need honest friends and mentors as you embark on a life-changing journey.

Just recently I had to break the news to someone that while his writing showed real promise, he needed to develop his craft more before quitting his day job to write the novel he'd been dreaming of. Many people dream of publishing a novel, and some decide to ditch everything else for the dream. If a person is ready, then maybe it's time to ditch everything. But the wife of this particular man, out of his line of vision, mouthed "Thank you" to me after I'd convinced her husband to give his development more time before loading it with the pressure to succeed and pay off. During our discussion it had become apparent that she was trying her best to be supportive while hiding her panic. Fortunately her husband had sought a professional assessment before plunging into a major life shift.

Balance Is Not Necessarily Safety

Sometimes you do have to take big risks. Comedienne Carol Burnett headed for Hollywood with a few thousand dollars in her pocket, given by a man in the entertainment industry who recognized her gifts. The amount was a lot for those days, but it wasn't enough to support her for very long. He'd simply supplied her with the opportunity to take a good shot at a career in show business. She took that shot and paid him back before very long—and thus began a long and successful life of using her gifts.

Balance does not mean that you always do the safe thing. Many of us in the creative arts do that work at the expense of a better income. I could easily work full time as an editor; I could probably make a good living editing and writing under freelance assignment. We could pay off our mortgage sooner, could buy a nicer car. But Jim and I have both made choices according to not only financial necessities but our gifts and opportunities. We're both doing what we are gifted to do, to one degree or another, and in order to do that we operate without much, if any, financial cushion. This is our choice, and from time to time we have to open yet another discussion about all of the needs vying for our attention and our bank account.

Sometimes you do pack your car and head for a new city with no clear plan, just an overwhelming conviction that this is the right thing at the right time. People make such moves for many reasons other than art. I know families that live on the edge for the sake of taking God's love to people in precarious situations, whether through providing medical relief in a faraway country or staffing an inner-city church. People who live by strong convictions are usually the most balanced folks you'll find; their lives are rarely "safe," but their kind of balance works just fine.

I headed for a two-year teaching assignment in the Middle East back when a high school superintendent was holding a teaching position for me close to my parents' town. It was a good position in possibly the best school district in our region. I didn't even tell my parents that the position had been offered until I got my confirmation for the Middle East assignment; at that time the safety of a secure job close by was too important to them. A few years later I packed a used car with everything it would hold and set out for graduate school in Chicago in order to change careers entirely. At age thirty—which felt pretty old at the time—I was shifting gears because by then I knew that writing must have a much higher priority than a music education career allowed.

But once I acquired the graduate degree that opened doors in publishing, I had to do the safe thing for several years, doing full-time plus freelance work, walking alongside my husband who was fighting through a scary depression. That was the season for getting bills paid and finding the right doctors and medications, for stabilizing my marriage and home. Back then the safe thing was the necessary thing.

Sometimes you will take risks, and sometimes you will take the safer course. In the grand scheme of your life, if you are making wise decisions, acting out of love and vision, the balance will be there. But the larger balance often looks like imbalance in the day-to-day.

Anyone who has brought up children understands how slowly the balance can shift. For years you have to steal moments, an hour here or there, a weekend when you're lucky, to pay attention to your creative work, while another very creative work absorbs most of your energy—helping little people get a good start in life. Although I hear people talk wistfully of how little creative work they could do when their kids were small, I don't believe any of them think they shouldn't have made those choices, shouldn't have put off some things for the sake of nurturing children. And many creatives find a way to nurture their gifts even when the kids are underfoot. Madeleine L'Engle did a lot of her writing at one o'clock in the morning during the years when her children were young. She is one of the most dedicated writers I've ever met. But you have only to read some of her nonfiction, much of which revolves around her family, to see how dedicated she remained as a wife, a mother, a grandmother and a friend. She jokes about mopping the kitchen floor once every few months whether it needed it or not. In her life a messy house or a sticky floor did not represent imbalance; it represented proper priorities.

Balance Is Not Necessarily Consistency

Balance does not always mean that you have a stable schedule. My writing schedule shifts according to the time of year and the freelance assignments I've taken on. My freelance work is now determined by my writing goals, whereas years ago the freelance had to take preeminence. When the season changes, my writing shifts schedule and location in the house according to how the light is. In winter months I generally write in the living room, because there are more windows and it doesn't feel as oppressive as our small bedroom with one window. During the summer I often write late at night on the back porch, because it's quiet and dark in a full, peaceful way that tends to give my writing energy.

I work part time as an editor, and I go to the publishing company's office to do the editing. I may shift my writing days according to the publishing schedule. When there are doctor appointments or visitors during the week, I write more on the weekend.

All of this to say, I've probably never kept the same writing schedule for longer than a few weeks at a time. If I let that inconsistency bother me, my writing would have dried up a long time ago. I've accepted now that I will always work okay with a shifting schedule. I guess I'm a fickle personality in general, and I respond emotionally to a lot of variables that wouldn't affect other people. Some days my creative energy must find release in cooking, and that shifts my writing schedule. Some weekends I write many hours because I did considerable cooking during the week. Because cooking is a creative act for me, I don't consider it lost time, but I do try to make up the time I wasn't writing. So I dance from one day to the next, one week to the next, concentrating simply on getting the writing done.

What is a balanced life for you may not appear balanced to other people. That's not your problem. You can find a healthy balance, but it takes flexibility and willingness to live with uncertainty.

And emotional or spiritual balance is often not what it appears to be. A person who is quite balanced emotionally may still experience significant highs and lows in the course of creative engagement. There's nothing wrong with being sad or angry or silly; sometimes your work will do weird things with your emotions, but that's all part of the work itself and nothing to get upset about. You can't work with soul material day in and day out and maintain a placid, in-control emotional life. You can learn to embrace those emotions and take what they offer to your work.

If you think that spiritual balance is represented by a calm sort of life, I urge you to read about the spiritual geniuses across the centuries. Just about anyone who has made a positive spiritual impact on the world endured a good deal of "imbalance." Many of our spiritual heroes dealt with depression, oppression, poverty and failure. They would laugh at what we attempt to achieve today in the name of balance. Spirituality by nature is a pretty wild endeavor. You will frequently be in the land of unknowing.

In addition, your heightened sensitivity will be hard on you as you become more mindful of other people and their struggles, whether they are family members struggling with illness or people halfway around the world facing civil war. Your artistic gifts will enable you to experience more acutely the sadness and anger along with the joy and peace that are supposedly the hallmarks of spiritual maturity.

Spiritual growth guarantees imbalance of all sorts. One day you'll have faith, the next you'll feel covered in doubt. One day you will see God, the next day you'll doubt that God exists. This is called pilgrimage. It's also called growth. People who do not experience ups and downs and who do not struggle with life on a regular basis are not balanced; they are more likely stagnant.

Balance does not mean that you will always exercise the same set of creative gifts. At this point in my life, my calling is to write novels and some nonfiction. I don't assume that I will always do this, although it's fine with me if I do. If I wake up one day and realize that it's time to learn how to master screenplays or to start singing again or to learn something else entirely, then I will follow that calling too.

Make room for the possibility of multiple gifts in your life. Many people start out doing one thing and then uncover abilities to do others. It's easier to discover an ability after you have attained confidence in another one. Your creative development in one area will likely trigger the development of some other talent down the line.

Creativity brings tension with it. It will stretch you, because it is in creativity's nature to stretch people. You are constantly adjusting—when you change jobs, change towns or bring children into your life. You will also need to adjust when your gifts start leaning on your life and teaching you things.

The thing to remember is that the balance society often urges upon you has never existed, and it's a grand waste of your time and energy to seek it. Your balance will come with each new day, each thoughtful decision and each revelation that comes with your work.

THE LIGHT THAT HOLDS THE SOUL

It's important to acknowledge the darkness that comes with the wonder of creativity. But we can't neglect to celebrate the brightness. Creativity unveils. It reveals truth. It brings important matters to light. It gives us new sight of old topics. It unseals a box somewhere, and joy flies out into the fresh air. This soul space, in which you re-create some wonder that the Creator has already placed in the universe, is a very bright place in which to live.

If you value what is true, then you will find much light in the creative life. If you fear honesty, if you avoid the truth, then creativity will become a struggle. The work that unveils what is true cannot be tripped up by your nervousness about reality. The truth is bright, sometimes so bright that it hurts your eyes.

But truth brings healing and freedom. Once you draw all that material up out of the well, you are faced with the contents of your reality. And usually you must deal with the wounds first—the darkness. Your soul will take you to those hard matters, because God has designed you to long for and find healing.

Once you face the darkness, you will understand how to bring beauty out of it. You will hold the shining key to a particular character, or you will find the right perspective for that watercolor. You will see your fear for what it is and know how to portray it honestly in the poem or photograph. You will connect the problem with the solution, even if what you've discovered is one small part of the problem and solution.

Entertain the notion that your creative journey—through all sorts of trials and joys, well-lit places and pitch-black ones—is being held ultimately by a great light. This light holds your soul. And it will carry you through everything—through the dark places, through your development as an artist and your growth as a person. After all, if you are called to create, if this creative work is something you feel you must do, then the requirements of the work must be possible and ultimately good and satisfying for you.

✺ EXERCISES FOR A WRITER'S FORMATION

Essay About Darkness

Write a three-page essay that explores the darkness you have either found in your creative work or feared you would find there. Write quickly and don't edit. Then set it aside for a few days.

Now go back to the essay and work with it. Make sure it flows well and would be understandable to someone who knows nothing about you. Be certain to explain the terms and phrases you introduce. Come up with some sort of structure and revise accordingly. Leave it for a couple of days.

Go back to the revised essay and read it as though you were a counselor or simply a good friend. Insert comments into the essay, responses to what you find there. Suggest actions the writer might take. Offer encouragement, insight, whatever you think will help this person move forward in the creative work. Address fears and help the writer look more objectively at statements, memories and assumptions.

Worst-Case Scenarios

The phrase or sentence I most fear writing down or saying is . . .

The secret I most fear coming to light is . . .

The emotion that frightens me most is . . .

The location associated with my darkest moment is . . .

The failure that would shatter me most is . . .

The biggest mistake I could make is . . .

The cruelest thing I've ever said or done was . . .

My greatest regret so far is . . .

The one thing I dread more than anything is . . .

The possibility I worry about most is . . .

The thing I need to do but can't is _____, and I think this is why:

The one person or event that can make me the angriest in the shortest amount of time is _____, and I think this is why:

The grief that won't let me go is . . .

Great writers always gave us a picture of a much larger world. They were never prisoners of their own skins. Even Emily Dickinson, the most socially isolated writer in America, even her writing is never self-conscious. She is never sitting in her tiny room narrating her own feelings.

GARRISON KEILLOR, IN *OF FICTION AND FAITH*

Dogmatists of all kinds—scientific, economic, moral, as well as political—are threatened by the creative freedom of the artist. This is necessarily and inevitably so. We cannot escape our anxiety over the fact that the artists together with creative persons of all sorts, are the possible destroyers of our nicely ordered systems. For the creative impulse is the speaking of the voice and the expressing of the forms of the preconscious and unconscious; and this is, by its very nature, a threat to rationality and external control.

ROLLO MAY, *THE COURAGE TO CREATE*

These artists emphasize that personal and spiritual growth results from diligently focusing on a particular set of activities over an extended period of time. . . . Paradoxically, these artists insist that their ability to create is enhanced by following a well-established set of procedures.

ROBERT WUTHNOW, *CREATIVE SPIRITUALITY*

If you choose the riskier path and decided to spend your life as a creator, you have the job of feeling successful no matter what your objective successes look like. You must train yourself to feel successful, despite what your heart and the world tell you about your lack of success.

ERIC MAISEL, *THE VAN GOGH BLUES*

9   THE HOME BUILT
IN EXILE

*How to Thrive as a Creative
in the Real World*

One of the best things that ever happened to me was junior-high
English class with Mrs. Lundquist. Nearly all that I learned about
grammar—until I became an editor and learned it on the job—was acquired in seventh grade. For years I kept the back section of that English workbook because it had all the "Keys," the grammar rules and
examples. I never encountered anything that helpful in high school or
college.

Mrs. Lundquist submitted my poetry to *Read Magazine,* a monthly
that was used in language arts back then. My first published words appeared in *Read.* When the magazine sponsored a nationwide contest
for young short story writers, Mrs. Lundquist made certain that I finished a story and entered it.

One day, weeks after the school secretary had typed up my story
and Mrs. Lundquist had sent it to the national office, I was sick at
home. During my grammar school career I clocked a lot of sick days,
and teachers were accustomed to sending my homework to me when
I couldn't be in class. But this day there was a knock on the door, and

I crept down the hallway to see Dad talking out on the front stoop with our principal. After he left, Dad told me that I needed to go to the school. He and Mom took me, and I landed in Mrs. Lundquist's room while my parents waited in the principal's office. Mrs. Lundquist talked for a while about an assignment or two I'd missed, or something like that; it was rather vague, and I was pretty confused. In the middle of our discussion, I was called to the office.

When I walked in, someone handed me the telephone. The person on the other end was calling from some distant city to congratulate me on winning first place in the eighth-grade division of the short story contest. I don't remember a word of that conversation; when the person (male or female? I don't remember) asked what had brought me to write the particular story I'd submitted, I managed to say something like, "Well, I had to come up with something."

I would receive a gold medal and a savings bond worth five hundred dollars. In exchange, the Xerox Corporation would own my story.

I lived in Cherokee, Kansas, population nine hundred or so. My story had placed over possibly a thousand others from all over the country. My picture appeared in local papers with a paragraph describing my victory. I'm pretty sure it was displayed at the tavern where my grandpa spent many of his evenings.

You'd think that I would have grabbed hold of that, would have said that very day, "I'm going to be a writer." You'd think that when I showed the story to the doctor in charge of my kidneys, up at Kansas University Medical Center, and she sent me a personal letter praising it and included a book of Emily Dickinson poems, I would have claimed my place in the literary world.

But we didn't know any writers. We had no money to invest in anything that wasn't a sure thing. I was able to attend college thanks only to federal grants; today I would be out of luck. I had been playing piano since age six. I would become a music teacher; this I never questioned. It would be decades before I created any semblance of a writing life.

For many people a whole world, or a powerful aspect of their world, stands in the way of living out their gifts. It's hard to be creative in a land of bottom lines, political campaigns, religious wars, the strip mall, adult supervision, corporately sponsored education, opinion polls, sexual repression/excess, Palm Pilots, high anxiety and two-hour commutes. It's hard to discover your gifts and nurture them to maturity when you have no names for them and when most social structures have no place for them.

Your development—creative formation—is really up to you. Others may offer help and encouragement, but the bulk of what must be done issues from your own soul, where all the visions begin and where God's voice is most clearly heard.

You need a home, a safe place in which to grow and nurture your gifts. It can help to think of your creative self as a person in exile. You must carry "home" within you and work with the outer particulars as best you can.

✐ THE PHYSICAL PARTICULARS: TIME, SPACE AND EQUIPMENT

I have no new ideas about creating time and space for creativity. You most likely live with other people, and you may be responsible for several of them—children or other dependents. You may have no choice but to work full time at a job that doesn't involve your gifts. You, like all creative people before and after you, must juggle multiple loves or, at the very least, multiple obligations. Your dilemma is nothing new.

Time Is Limited, but Recognize Options
Limited time and limited energy are partners; you rarely have one without the other. What you must come to is a series of choices about what energy you will offer to your time.

You will have to sacrifice less important things for creative callings. You will probably watch less TV, sleep late less often, not party quite as much and let go of other tasks and projects. You may not get that home improvement done for another six months or another year. You may turn down more weekend excursions. These are your choices. While you must often give up activities that you enjoy, be careful not to give up the activities that engage you with life and give you not only energy but creative fuel.

You can manage creative time much better once you decide that creativity is flexible enough to have its way at various times of the day and in various situations. If you have small children, your creativity will have to learn how to click on whenever they are asleep or in someone else's care. It's better if you can stick to some sort of schedule, but children often don't, so the Muse will just have to operate in a less finicky fashion than it would if you had more options or fewer responsibilities.

Believe it or not, you have significant "dead time" in your day. For me for several years, it was the train commute during which I wrote significant portions of two novels. I had enough juice early in the morning and right after work to keep functioning and get work done, forty minutes at a time.

Many Americans routinely don't get enough sleep, but if you're one of those people who manage to sleep in quite a bit, you might consider holding yourself to sleeping only seven or eight hours five nights of the week and doing your creative work at either the beginning or the end of your day. You may not even miss the sleep.

Back when I was working full time, I fashioned mini-retreats for myself a couple of times per year. I would set aside two or three days, usually long weekends, when I let everything else go and concentrated on my writing. There are times when the work needs a longer span of uninterrupted time. Those short writing retreats really did compensate for my overall abbreviated writing schedule, which usually amounted to only a couple of hours per day and some days not even that.

Although many artists say that you must do creative work every day, I am proof that you can do decent work in patches. I don't write every day. I look forward to a time when I can. But now I am still working as an editor part time, so most of my writing happens on three days of the week, plus parts of weekends. This works for me. You can discover what works for you. Many people have trouble doing any kind of creative work in the space of an hour here or there. I encourage you to look at all the different tasks that make up your work and figure out which of them is easier to get into quickly. For instance, I can click into editing mode pretty quickly, so I often self-edit when I have only an hour or so. I prefer a longer period for my creative-flow, free-writing work. But I can also free write in a short time. The beauty of free writing is that there are no rules, so I can work on a scene for merely fifteen minutes if that's all the time I have.

Find exercises that tap your creativity quickly, and use them when you don't have much time. This is why it's important to load yourself with a large bag of creative practices. The more practices you have, the more flexible you can be. You'll be surprised at how much work you can do even when you don't have large blocks of time.

Use all of your other time—your ordinary, "noncreative" time—to engage with your creativity. Be a sponge, and absorb all the daily tasks and small events, storing up material or simply strong emotion for later use. Some people carry a journal for this purpose, but even if you don't record what's happening, you will benefit creatively if you merely attend to life more consciously as it happens.

If you can, find other people to do your maintenance work. Although I've never dedicated long hours to housework, I've always tried to keep my home clean and organized enough that we can find things and have space to do what we want. Even though I may only spend a few hours per week on that maintenance work, concern about it can crowd my creative space. So about two years ago, after I had cut back to part-time salaried work, I hired someone to clean my house every other week. It doesn't cost a fortune, and the need for a clean house is one less worry crowding my thoughts. I often use the few hours the cleaning person is here to do other sorting and straightening, paying bills and so forth. But the anxiety is gone, and I'm not tempted to sacrifice writing time for an hour to vacuum the house. I wonder why it took me so long to take this simple yet effective step.

Jim and I also decided to hire people to do some of the home improvement projects we've been trying to get to for years. I would like to learn how to be handier at home decorating and repair, but I have to choose where my time is best spent. How many writing days would I lose once I got into the flow of fixing and painting? How many weekends would get eaten up? So I've chosen to have this work done by others. It will cost some money, but for me, lost time is more costly.

Some tasks just have to wait. For months I've wanted to go through drawers of photographs and mementos to organize and store them, but they just don't have high enough priority to displace my creative time. As much as the creative cook in me would love to put on a banquet several times a month, I often choose to make tuna sandwiches— and sometimes grab takeout—rather than spend two to three hours on a given day making lists, grocery shopping, cooking and then cleaning up the mess.

Sit down with yourself and make your choices. What is really important to you? If you struggle with what kind of priority your creative work should have, then skip right now to a later section in this chapter: "The Psychological Particulars."

Space Is at a Premium, but Be Flexible

If you write or engage in some other creative work that doesn't require much space, then you're one of the lucky ones. You can turn one small corner of your house into your writing space. In fact, you can have several writing spaces, depending on the time of year or day. The less stuff you have, the better. Try to be as mobile as possible; be one backpack away from a writing afternoon. If you wait until you have a nice office space where you can store all your equipment, books, music and wall hangings, you may never have that physical space. What a foolish reason to neglect your gifts.

I've learned to gather my stuff according to project. Sometimes it's a file folder or a sturdy box; other times it's a grocery sack or canvas bag: I keep the notes and everything that has to do with a particular project together. That way I can just pick up that box or bag and go to any spot and work. I'll even store pens and other supplies in each bag so that I don't have to go on a pen search every time I switch projects.

I've also learned to look at my time realistically and take only what I really need. I rarely write and do research reading in the same session. So I don't drag a stack of books with me whenever I'm writing. I'll do my reading some other time. You may not work this way, but it's important that you figure out how you work and organize your space and stuff accordingly.

Even though you usually have more options than are visible at first, you can't do creative work just anywhere. There are aspects of your workspace that merit attention.

Light. Whether it's natural light, soft light or indirect light, arrange your space so that you have the lighting that works for you. I prefer writing with some natural light in the room, but I don't like a bright space because the light competes with my laptop screen. So I'll often write in a room near a window but with no other lights on. You may really need daylight for your emotional well-being, especially if you suffer from seasonal affective disorder (SAD). You can now buy lights that will give you the equivalent of sunlight all year round. Get whatever you need. Not only will your eyes hold up better, but you'll simply feel better and less stressed if you have the proper lighting.

Comfortable workspace. It makes sense to spend money on a decent chair and/or work surface. If you are physically uncomfortable, you will unconsciously come up with all sorts of ways to sabotage your creative time. If you can't get comfortable, it will be more difficult for you to get into the creative flow or to stay engaged for long. This also comes under the next section, "Equipment," but it is crucial to your physical space.

Organized storage. "Organized" means many things to many people. You know what it means for you. Whether you are quite particular about where things are kept or you work comfortably with piles of stuff that frighten other humans, you need to manage clutter so that it doesn't get in the way of your work. You can build expensive shelves, buy nice furniture, buy twenty milk crates, or have a corner full of bags and file boxes. But for your own sake, put things where you can find them and where they won't bother you when you're not working on them. How much they bother the people you live with is another matter, and you'll have to negotiate as best you can.

Comfort items. For me, comfort is a pot of something hot to drink. Sometimes it's music in the background. Do what you can to give your space small touches that make it yours, if only for a couple of hours per day when the kids are at school or when everyone else is in bed or watching TV. There may be some object that is a sort of icon for you. You might want pictures of loved ones around you. You may want a few books or works of art that give you inspiration. A certain little throw rug or afghan may make you feel warmer and more ready to entertain the Muse. You may need a little vase of flowers or a candle. Most of these things aren't expensive or hard to come by. Make your space inviting, because you want to look forward to being there.

If your creative work requires a lot of space or large equipment, the only advice I have is that you seek out someone else with those same needs and see if you can share a studio, a darkroom, whatever. There are a number of people out there trying to do work that is similar to yours, and most of them aren't so well off that they wouldn't appreciate another artist to share both the space and the expense.

But even work that requires significant space can be possible right where you are. One friend of mine who makes masks and sculptures has set apart an area of his basement. Other people partition off space in the garage, or they finish attic space enough to work there. You may be able to make space for yourself simply by sorting and pitching for a day or two and freeing up space that has been used mainly for storage.

Equipment Is Necessary, but Take the Frugal Approach

Once you've decided that you're called to create, it can be tempting to run out and spend a lot of money outfitting yourself for this new artsy life. Please don't. A big debt at the outset of a creative season just adds more pressure. It's not wise when you're learning a new sport to buy the most high-end equipment before you've even managed the basics. You hope that you'll learn the skills and stick with it, but until you've established some pretty firm patterns, less expensive—or even used—equipment will work just fine.

When I first began to write consistently for pay, I knew that I would not be able to work at my distant office at a desk and computer and then come home and sit at my own desk and computer to write creatively. My energy wouldn't take it; my back and neck wouldn't take it. I had a perfectly fine computer and desk at home, but what I needed was a laptop that I could take with me on the train. I also needed a chair in which I could sit with my laptop in the early mornings or in the evenings at home.

Having been given a modest advance for the first novel, I used part of it to buy a used laptop. It was a couple of years old, which in the computer world is way behind the times. But it processed words and sentences just fine. It had enough memory to manage possibly two novels at once. I used this laptop for nearly four years. It had its glitches, but it served the purpose. Eventually, when I had better cash flow and when this laptop was wearing out, I bought a new one, which I'll probably use until it wears out.

We also bought a small, overstuffed recliner to put in one corner of our bedroom. This has been my writing chair for several years. In the mid-recline position, my legs are up far enough that the laptop is at a comfortable level but I am not horizontal enough to get sleepy. I can sit there for hours a day and write without getting cramps. We invested a few hundred dollars in the chair, at a time when a few hundred dollars was not just sitting in our bank account. But it was an investment in my creative work.

Fortunately, writing doesn't require many large investments. Whatever your creative work is, it will bring its own requirements. But don't assume that you need all the equipment right now or that you must have everything new or have the most cutting-edge machinery. It's wise to build up equipment as you build your creative life; you increase the physical components as the interior development calls for them. If you spend thousands of dollars before you've built much of a creative life, it's easy to feel that you must make that life pay off, and soon. Don't put this kind of pressure on yourself.

Once you have your physical particulars, feel free to get protective of them. My husband usually checks with me before he uses my laptop. The children in my life, who are generally free to wreck the rest of the house, know that they're in trouble the minute they approach the laptop. Although I love my "stuff," I try to keep a loose hold on most physical possessions. The laptop, where virtually all my writing happens, is the chief exception.

⚜ THE PSYCHOLOGICAL PARTICULARS: CONVICTION, FAITH AND VISION

If you find that you're having trouble with time, space and equipment, you may not be fully convinced yet that you have the right to invest in your creative callings. You haven't given yourself permission to embrace the work. This permission doesn't happen once and for all; you end up saying yes many times. Although the following three divisions are artificial, they mark three possible aspects that "yes" might manifest for you.

Conviction Says Yes to the Work

Can you name the work that is calling you? Can you put yourself in some category? Maybe you're simply a writer but you can't be any more specific than that. This is fine. Some writers start out as short story writers and end up as poets, or start as poets and end up as something else. You figure it out in stages. You may have a strong sense of the specific work that is yours, but most people who commit themselves to their gifts discover eventually that they will do more than one kind of work.

How do you gain real conviction about this calling? First of all, you explain to yourself what the calling is *not*. I keep going back to a saying I heard years ago in church: God doesn't call you to be successful, only faithful. I think this is a perfect saying for every creative person to hold dear. You're called simply to do the work. You give your time and energy to the work. You can't worry about the outcome or how much money you'll make. You can't worry about other people's opinions of the work. What's important is your conviction to engage in the work.

Second, you explain to yourself that you are committing yourself to the work, period—not to a lifestyle or a schedule. You may not be able to give many hours to your creativity right away. You are convinced, however, that you will develop this part of your life. If the development amounts to just an hour or so every week or a weekend every month, then that's something.

You are not committing yourself to an "artsy" lifestyle either. You may not even be the artsy type. You may read and write poetry but do little else that would set you apart as the creative type. You don't have to start dressing in black or watching certain kinds of films. You don't need to hold particular political opinions or keep company with different friends. Your commitment is to the development of creativity, in whatever form it will take in your personality and circumstances.

All you're doing in saying yes is accepting that you have work to do and deciding to participate in it more fully and intentionally than you have until now. This simple conviction will make all the difference. It may not be a visible difference, except to a few people who are close to you.

Faith Says Yes to the Process

So now that you've decided to engage in creative work, what will happen to you? Nobody knows! You need a bit of faith now to just get with the process and trust it to do good things in your life.

A process is not static; you will be moving, shifting, dancing for balance from now on. You will never know it all. You will never see far into your own future. Can you say yes to this kind of life? Yes is possible once you decide to trust the process, once you don't require everything in black and white. When you say yes to process, you say goodbye to certainty, which is just as well, because most certainty is false anyway.

A process requires that you go in one direction or another. Either you learn or you regress. Either you adjust or you atrophy. When you say yes to the process, you are also expressing some faith in your own potential, in your ability to grow and learn and change. If you have trouble trusting this, then look back a few decades and review what you have survived so far. Talk to loved ones who can remind you of how strong you have already been and how much you have already learned and accomplished.

When you say yes to the process, you are saying, "I can do this—but I don't have to do it all today or do it perfectly." Process implies gradual development. It implies trial and error, failures that teach and struggles that strengthen. So, even if you can't imagine yourself sticking with your writing work until a whole novel is finished, you can imagine writing a good scene sometime within the next month. This kind of faith says yes to the process.

Vision Says Yes to the Dream

Are you willing to attempt a work that is beyond your abilities? Are you game for challenges that will make your life crazy—but richer and wiser? Within a process that leads you step by step, can you afford to take some risks? Such commitment requires vision. Some creative folks start with vision, while some of us take time to work up to it.

I've never been the ambitious type. Oh yes, I daydream about writing the novel that gets turned into a movie that wins the Academy Award for Best Picture, but I don't set upon my days and weeks as if any such thing might actually happen. I was the last person to believe that my creative gifts merited my cutting back on a "real" job in order to write more; it seemed so unrealistic. Other people had visions for me long before I did. So if you don't have visions yet, don't worry. You can still commit yourself to the creative life. You can say yes to the work and yes to the process. The visions will come as you gain some confidence in your abilities. As you engage in the work, you will learn to trust your dreams more. You will begin to give yourself more permission to have dreams.

Vision will set higher goals for you than you might naturally set for yourself. Vision will enable you to embark on a work that has no practical purpose that you can see right now. Vision will help you keep working when the work is hard or boring. And vision will give other people hope—and will often obtain partners in dreaming for you. My present vision is of a retreat house for writers. I'm beginning to talk about it more. I have no financial means to create such a thing, but if I entertain the vision, who knows what resources may pop up? For all I know, someone with land or a huge house is looking for a worthy cause to give it to. Or there's a group of other writers who are already working on such a project. But if I don't allow myself the vision, there's no way for me to even look into the possibilities or recognize them when they're right in front of me.

Visions don't always represent the true goal or the reality of your future. Some visions simply give us excellent practice in dreaming. Some novels remain unpublishable yet take our writing another step further so that we become ready to write the novels that will find a broader audience. When you commit yourself to dreams and visions, you are accepting that they won't all materialize. It's not up to you to make all those dreams and visions come true. But when you say yes to them, when you entertain them and go after them, they do amazing work inside you. They bring your skills along; they sharpen your intuition; they increase your excitement about life.

Conviction says yes to the work itself. Faith says yes to the process that will continually form your soul and your gifts. Vision says yes to the dream that will stretch you and brighten your whole life.

Spend some time with these ideas. What yes are you ready for? Any yes can start out as a small step, and a small step is enough for now.

⁌ FAITH, ATTENTIVENESS AND CELEBRATION

Faith figures into creative work at every step. You say yes to the work, trusting that you are in some way called to it. You must have faith that you heard right and that there's an overarching reason for you to write stories or dance or build musical instruments. In faith you take an idea and run with it. You follow a hunch, or you take a moment to record a chance conversation, sensing that there's something there to return to later and develop.

In faith you stick with a project even as it changes shape while you're working on it. You believe that this shape will find itself eventually. You walk in faith as you rework a plot line for the fifth time and while you solve all sorts of problems that appear without notice. You work in faith as you see shadows of your idea appear in the works of others and you begin to fear that by the time you're finished someone else will have beaten you to the book deal or the art exhibit. You keep working and believing as you see public interest ebb and flow all around what you're trying to do.

You keep working in faith when your soul grows weary and the doubts increase. You keep the faith on the days you question your judgment and abilities and wonder if maybe you should just work in a coffee shop or do some mindless desk job and forget about the dreams and visions.

You even exercise faith when you finish a project and say goodbye to it. You remain in faith while you wait to see what the world will make of what you have done. While you hear rumors of disapproval and dissent, you maintain that regardless of what anybody says or surmises, you have done the work you were called to do. Maybe you did it imperfectly—certainly it didn't turn out exactly as you'd planned—

but you did it and it's finished now, and you will wait to see what the next project will be.

Faith is not a luxury in the creative life; it is the fuel that keeps the work moving.

Attentiveness, too, must be a constant companion. Your job as an artist is first of all to pay attention. Only when you do that will you perceive what is waiting to be revealed and then interpreted to the rest of the world. You attend to every detail that presents itself. You gather information and work with it until you make meaning out of it. This attentiveness is intrinsic to every part of your process. First you pay attention to the signals, to see what work you are to do. Then you attend to how all the pieces relate to each other. You play with them and work with them and notice everything about them until you understand how you are to shape them.

Just about everything you notice in the course of your work is visible to other people too. The difference is that you take the time, the stillness, the energy, the curiosity and the thoughtfulness to examine what others pass by. You study a building's silhouette, meditate on it and come up with ways of describing it. Its shadow may become part of a background you are painting, or its presence may become a character in a scene you're writing. To most other folks it's just a building they walk past on the way to work. To you, that one building can become any number of things.

You also pay attention to your inner environment. You make it a point to be aware of the sensations you experience and the pattern your thoughts take. You remember dreams, write paragraphs on your emotional state, turn little bits of family history into a story line. And you come to respect yourself as an immense source of wisdom and inspiration. Your ordinary life begins to bloom into all sorts of possibilities for revelation.

Your primary job as an artist is to seduce other people into paying attention. You are not creating anything new; you are re-creating what already exists so that people will recognize it and deal with it.

You describe activities and name states of being so that the people who witness your work will have a fuller vocabulary for their own life. You help people see what has been in front of them all along. You help them remember what has been buried so deep that they couldn't find it on their own. You enable them to see themselves a little more clearly.

What about celebration? Is that what you do when the final draft is complete or when the play is finally produced? Of course, the final stage of a creative work calls for celebration. But if you wait until the end to celebrate, you will be tempted to hurry through the rest of the process in order to get there. Like faith and attentiveness, celebration must be present at every step of the journey.

You celebrate when you get that first idea. You have no idea how the project will end up, but for now the idea is glorious, and how fortunate you are to have stumbled upon it. All of the giddy emotions and the anxiety and excitement of the beginning are worth their own celebration. You have something to do! You have work taking shape before your eyes!

Celebrate the joy that comes simply because you are creating. Enjoy that first-draft rush of exuberance. Whenever I first put something into words, it just seems miraculous; it reads so beautifully, and I appear to myself to be utterly talented. All the while I know, deeper down, that this first draft is going to look like exactly that when my excitement settles down and I take a colder look at it. But for the moment I rejoice in the act of creating. I know that soon enough the joy will subside and I'll be left with loads of work to do. That doesn't prevent me from celebrating the present moment.

The whole long process of working and reworking, of revising and problem solving, is worthy of celebration. You have been given the privilege to work on this idea, this project. Ahead of you are days and days of engagement with your gifts. Days and days of learning and paying attention and discovering wisdom and beauty. Days and days of doing what you are gifted to do. One friend of mine said, years ago, of her struggles as a writer: "I have good problems. For instance, I get to work on this poem all morning. That's a good problem."

Celebration has to do with joy, and joy is linked to your gifts. Do not deny this joy. Receive it at every step for what it is. Celebrate where you are in your journey, whether you're just a babe trying to learn grammar or you have just completed your twentieth book. You are not celebrating success. You're not even celebrating your own genius. You are celebrating the fact that you get to be part of this marvelous process at all.

DWELLING IN YOUR CREATIVE HOME—AND OUT IN THE REST OF THE WORLD

Dominic is an author of mine, meaning that I've edited four of his books. He's a parish priest on the north side of Chicago, and he tells a fine story. He has a wonderful sense of the natural story that bubbles up in life every day, sometimes many times a day.

He also reads a lot of books, many of them novels. And when *Velma Still Cooks in Leeway* came out, my employers at Loyola Press (where I'm an editor) held a little celebration, giving me the opportunity to sign books there at the office. One of my fellow editors made sure Dominic got a copy.

It was a month or two before I had occasion to see Dominic again. In the meantime he'd read *Velma*. His reaction was a flood of enthusiasm. He's one of my best publicists, because he keeps recommending the book to people. He summed up his assessment with "After reading the last line I sobbed like a baby." This is my goal, to make grown men weep; it helps that Dom is a demonstrative Italian. Then a few moments later he said, almost as an afterthought, "You know, the way I felt reading *Velma* was the same way I felt years ago when I read *To Kill a Mockingbird*."

Sometimes grace just shows up, huge and bright, and blinds you to tears. After I recovered from Dom's comment, I revealed to him the critical role that *To Kill a Mockingbird* had played in my journey.

It took a few years, but I have created the writing life that started as adolescent heartbreak over the written word. Now I form the scenes and introduce the characters. What agony I have spent, and what the revelation has done to me.

What about you? Perhaps you have made some commitment to creativity, to explore for a while, submit to the process and see what happens. Maybe your commitment is specifically connected to a vision or a dream. Either way, you are at a new level of attentiveness to your gifts and what they might produce. You have made the time, constructed the right physical environment and equipped yourself.

You have gathered a community. You may have a mentor or teacher who can come alongside as you develop your craft. You likely have some fellow creators with whom you can share woes and progress. You may truly appreciate the value of good criticism, and so you seek feedback and advice from people who have the credentials to give it.

The more energy and respect you give to your gifts, the more your gifts will give back to you. Those gifts will benefit other people as well. This artist's life will bring you into contact with human experience in more and different ways than you have envisioned.

As you engage in the creative work to which you are called, no matter what that work is or how visible it becomes, you will dwell more deeply and more comfortably in your own life. You will become more aware of yourself and of the world around you. You will think more and listen more. Your joy will acquire new layers, and you'll find much more to laugh about and cry about. As you participate in this life, something deep inside will feel more together, more integrated. You can step more firmly into your own life story, and although you will likely face many dangers and darknesses, you will find yourself less fearful and more daring, less anxious and yet more caring.

Perhaps you have begun to build the home in exile, the place that is safe for creativity and soul work, even when the surrounding environment is cluttered and noisy and threatening. You may have built that home out of sheer self-defense. No one else would make a place for you and your gifts, so you had to take it upon yourself to build a house and outfit it with furniture.

Such a home will become a haven, not just for you but for other pilgrims. So many people are desperate to rest and wait for some word from God, to find their gifts, express their experiences and explore their possibilities. Those people will find you as you establish your little home in exile. Some will just want a cup of coffee and an afternoon chat, while others may need to stay much longer, for healing and inspiration.

I've seen how imbalanced people become when they contain themselves within a religious subculture and avoid anything "outside." I've seen what fear of the unknown can do and the good work it can prevent. Most people who have embraced their creativity have had to sacrifice some safety. But once they face the unknown and travel outside the safe realm, they discover how strong their own gifts have made them. They also discover how much their gifts can nurture other people.

So in a strange sense, the person who is committed to creative callings is like a missionary. You have discovered how marvelous the world can be, because your gifts have developed your attentiveness, your ability to experience things. You hope that your novel or sculpture will help others see how wonderful the world is too. You want to see them relax as they get lost in the scene or song. You know what a good thing it is to partake deeply of life, and you want to live in a world where more and more people learn how to participate fully in their own life.

I dream that when people read my stories they will walk through the world with more hope and tenderness. I pray that my words help them ask important questions and speak what they know to be true. And I deeply desire that *you* will learn, every day, to say yes and risk what God might do within you through the revelatory process of creation. May this beautiful divinity—God the Creator as reflected in human creativity—be formed in your life, season after season.

✎ EXERCISES FOR A WRITER'S FORMATION

The Perfect Creating Environment

Imagine an object that represents your spiritual life. It can be a statue, a picture, a book, anything that can be held in the hand. Spend a few moments allowing this object to come into detail in your mind.

Now, finish this little story:

"One day [or night] I was given the miraculous ability to build a studio for my creative work. I began in the morning [or evening] and finished by nightfall [or daybreak]. Here's what happened:"

The only event that must be inserted into this story is that in the midst of the building you come across your object. It can arrive in any way: by special delivery, in an old shoebox you'd forgotten, in a particular drawer, stuck between magazines, hanging on a wall. You come across the object, and you incorporate it in your new studio—or not. If you incorporate it, be specific as to how. If you dispose of it or put it away somewhere else, be specific.

Did you know pretty quickly what your studio would look like?

Was building your studio a tense experience or an enjoyable one?

Were you surprised by anything in this story?

Was your spiritual object easy to include in the story?

How close to your actual creative space is the studio you just built in your imagination?

Compare your ideal studio with the space that you do have. What part of your dream is already a reality? What parts of it could you make a reality without much trouble or expense?

A Positive Voice

I need to find courage and strength to really claim my gifts. In order to do this, I must see a certain person and get this person's blessing. This is how I imagine doing that:

And this is what I imagine that person will say:

Negative Voices

There are three negative voices in my life; they discourage my living out my gifts. (These voices could be real people, the culture around you or your own inner critic.)

These are the three voices:

This is what each of those voices says:

And this is what I will say to each of the three in order to silence them:

Create a Plan

Devise a plan for your creative gifts over the next six months. Take stock of where you are in terms of faith, vision, goals and so on. Evaluate where you stand in terms of the development of your craft. Make lists of ideas you have for what to create.

Make the plan simple, something you can carry out. Assign yourself certain times and places in which to engage in your work. Determine the kinds of support you will need, and make plans to get the help of a friend or take a course. Spend an afternoon or a weekend creating a space in which to do your work. Write up some simple goals for yourself. Create a plan you can live with but that will challenge you.

APPENDIX

Using This Book with a Group

*B*ecause this book is structured topically, it should lend itself easily to group discussion. For the most part chapters can be dealt with in any order that suits the group, although I would advise following their order in the book. The leader can change from session to session, and no expertise is required. It would be helpful if the leader has had some experience in small group discussions. The purpose is to facilitate more than direct.

Some chapters are rather lengthy, and your group may prefer to spend two or three sessions in one chapter, covering one or two sections at a time. The group should read the text before discussing it, because the material will likely stir up memories, questions and ideas in the participants. If people don't have enough time to reflect after reading, the group discussion could be frustrating more than helpful.

At the end of this appendix is a set of twenty-seven questions, three per chapter, which can be used as discussion starters. But you are free to draw your own questions from the material, questions that best suit your particular group.

The group time should be structured loosely, to allow a free flow of ideas. With such topics there are no right or wrong answers. Invite participants to tell stories about how the element taken up in the chapter has worked itself out in their experiences.

You might have one person per session act as secretary, making lists of suggestions, ideas or questions to be explored in more detail later. With group discussion it's often helpful to use a flip chart or dry-erase board so that people can visualize the main points of discussion.

✒ WRITING EXERCISES

Any writing exercise has the potential for becoming quite personal, so take care when making exercises part of the group work. No one should ever feel pressured to read aloud anything he or she has written. If an exercise is to be shared with the group, make that clear and agree on it before anyone has written the exercise.

If the group is more than seven or eight people, it may work best to break into smaller groups of two or three to read what people have written. This allows more time per person and will feel less intimidating to some people.

The most helpful way to approach the writing exercises as a group may be to talk about the *experience* of doing the exercise, rather than reading what people have written in response to it. Much of *The Soul Tells a Story* is aimed at helping people understand their process; group discussion should reflect that aim to some degree.

If people want to read their exercises to one another, set ground rules about what sort of critique is called for. Most exercises in this book do not emphasize craft and should not be critiqued primarily for craft but rather for the content itself. Participants should help one another reflect on what their written responses indicate about their personal development.

For some sessions, you may want to assign people to choose a partner and work on a particular exercise before the next session. This should be presented as a suggestion to see how participants feel about it. Depending on the group, some of the best work may well happen outside group time with others who are in the group.

Periodically make the point that no one person will have a good experience with every exercise. If just a handful of exercises work for a participant, that's a good result. People should not be discouraged when an exercise does not go well; they can simply go on to another and find the one or two that are really helpful.

The small group should be a safe place for every person. Its purpose is to facilitate participants' walking alongside one another as they explore their individual path of creativity. If some participants want rigorous critique and frequent writing assignments, those activities would probably happen best in another group. The discussions from *The Soul Tells a Story* should help each person understand what kind of critique and support he or she needs and where to find it.

SUGGESTED QUESTIONS FOR GROUP DISCUSSION

Chapter 1: The Heart-Stopping Act of Saying Yes

What characteristics of creativity have already been recognizable in your life?

Who has named your gifts, and how did that happen?

When you say yes to the creative life, what are you personally saying yes to?

Chapter 2: The Journey of Creative Formation

How have creativity and spirituality been linked in your experience?

In what ways have creativity and spirituality been in conflict for you?

Which characteristics of creative formation are already present in your life?

Chapter 3: The Practices That Engage the Process

When did you first become aware that your creative work followed a process?

What is most difficult for you—the beginning, middle or end—and what have you done to get through that part?

What spiritual practices do you already know of, or use, that might apply well to creative work?

Chapter 4: The Various Ways We Tap the Well

Where do you go, or what do you do, to really get inspired?

What aspects of your well are most frightening or uninteresting to you?

Try to think of a way your creativity is linked to someone else in your family tree.

Chapter 5: The Balance That Leads to Greatness

Would you say that you are more left-brained or right-brained?

What part of the creative process is most unnatural to you?

Describe a time when you became acutely aware of your intuition.

Chapter 6: The Community That Counts

How has community supported your creative life?

When has community made your creative life painful or difficult?

What would you say is your most crucial community need right now, as a creative person?

Chapter 7: The Self You Must Face

Describe a shadow side of your gifts.

What part of your self do you feel least inclined to explore: history, family, experience, personality?

If you were to choose one aspect of your self on which to base a short story, what might it be?

Chapter 8: The Beauty and Danger of a Creative Life

At what point has pain been attached to your creative work?

Do you experience more darkness from within or from the people or situation around you?

Where have you gone to find healing while in the midst of creative work?

Chapter 9: The Home Built in Exile

Describe what seems to you the ideal creative life.

What is your next step in building your creative home?

Who do you visualize being with you as you work out your creative visions?

RESOURCES

Atwood, Margaret. *Negotiating with the Dead: A Writer on Writing.* Cambridge: Cambridge University Press, 2002.

Barron, Frank, and Alfonso Montuori and Anthea Barron. *Creators on Creating: Awakening and Cultivating the Imaginative Mind.* New York: Jeremy P. Tarcher/Putnam, 1997.

Barry, William A., and William J. Connolly. *The Practice of Spiritual Direction.* San Francisco: HarperSanFrancisco, n.d.

Bayles, David, and Ted Orland. *Art and Fear: Observations on the Perils (and Rewards) of Artmaking.* Santa Cruz, Calif.: Image Continuum, 1993.

Bradbury, Ray. *Zen in the Art of Writing: Essays on Creativity.* Santa Barbara, Calif.: Joshua Odell, 1994.

Brown, W. Dale. *Of Fiction and Faith: Twelve American Writers Talk About Their Vision and Work.* Grand Rapids: Eerdmans, 1997.

Bustard, Ned, ed. *It Was Good: Making Art to the Glory of God.* Baltimore: Square Halo, 2000.

Cameron, Julie. *The Artist's Way: A Spiritual Path to Higher Creativity.* New York: Jeremy P. Tarcher/Putnam, 1992.

Coupar, Regina. *The Art of Soul: An Artist's Guide to Spirituality.* Ottawa, Canada: Novalis, 2002.

Dillard, Annie. *The Writing Life.* New York: Harper & Row, 1989.

Fischer, Kathleen R. *The Inner Rainbow: The Imagination in Christian Life.* New York: Paulist, 1983.

Gardner, John. *The Art of Fiction: Notes on Craft for Young Writers.* New York: Vintage, 1985.

Goldberg, Natalie. *Writing Down the Bones.* Boston: Shambhala, 1986.

Hagberg, Janet O. *Wrestling with Your Angels: A Spiritual Journey to Great Writing.* Holbrook, Mass.: Adams, 1995.

Hansen, Ron. *A Stay Against Confusion: Essays on Faith and Fiction.* San Francisco: HarperCollins, 2001.

Hearne, Keith, and David Melbourne. *Understanding Dreams.* London: New Holland, 1999.

Hirsch, Edward. *The Demon and the Angel: Searching for the Source of Artistic Inspiration.* New York: Harcourt, 2002.

Jung, C. G. *Memories, Dreams, Reflections.* New York: Vintage, 1989.

Klauser, Henriette Anne. *Writing on Both Sides of the Brain: Breakthrough Techniques for People Who Write.* New York: Harper & Row, 1987.

Lamott, Anne. *Bird by Bird: Some Instructions on Writing and Life.* New York: Doubleday, 1994.

Laufer, Joanna, and Kenneth S. Lewis. *Inspired: The Breath of God—Conversations with Gifted People About Their Faith and Inspiration.* New York: Doubleday, 1998.

L'Engle, Madeleine. *Madeleine L'Engle [Herself]: Reflections on a Writing Life.* Comp. Carole F. Chase. Colorado Springs: Shaw/Waterbrook, 2001.

———. *Walking on Water: Reflections on Faith and Art.* 1980; reprint, Colorado Springs: Shaw/Waterbrook, 2001.

Leonard, Linda Schierse. *The Call to Create: Celebrating Acts of Imagination.* New York: Harmony, 2000.

Levoy, Gregg. *Callings: Finding and Following an Authentic Life.* New York: Three Rivers, 1997.

Maisel, Eric. *The Van Gogh Blues: The Creative Person's Path Through Depression.* Emmaus, Penn.: Rodale, 2002.

May, Rollo. *The Courage to Create.* New York: W. W. Norton, 1975.

Metcalf, Linda Trichter, and Tobin Simon. *Writing the Mind Alive: The Proprioceptive Method for Finding Your Authentic Voice.* New York: Ballantine, 2002.

O'Connor, Flannery. *Mystery and Manners: Occasional Prose.* New York: Farrar, Straus & Giroux, 1970.

Palmer, Helen, ed. *Inner Knowing: Consciousness, Creativity, Insight, Intuition.* New York: Jeremy P. Tarcher/Putnam, 1998.

Peters, Thomas C. *The Christian Imagination: G. K. Chesterton on the Arts.* San Francisco: Ignatius, 2000.

Rilke, Rainer Maria. *Letters to a Young Poet.* New York: W. W. Norton, 1993.

Ryken, Leland, ed. *The Christian Imagination: The Practice of Faith in Literature and Writing.* 1981; reprint, Colorado Springs: Shaw/Waterbrook, 2002.

Sayers, Dorothy L. *The Mind of the Maker.* San Francisco: HarperCollins, 1979.

Stein, Sol. *Stein on Writing.* New York: St. Martin's, 1995.

Stinissen, Wilfrid. *The Gift of Spiritual Direction: On Spiritual Guidance and Care of the Soul.* Liguori, Mo.: Liguori, 1999.

Turner, Steve. *Imagine: A Vision for Christians in the Arts.* Downers Grove, Ill.: InterVarsity Press, 2001.

Wakefield, Dan. *Releasing the Creative Spirit.* Woodstock, Vt.: Skylight Paths, 2001.

Wuthnow, Robert. *Creative Spirituality: The Way of the Artist.* Berkeley: University of California Press, 2001.

ABOUT THE AUTHOR

Vinita Hampton Wright is a critically acclaimed writer and professional editor who conducts creative formation workshops at conferences around the country. She is the author of three novels— *Grace at Bender Springs, Velma Still Cooks in Leeway* and *The Winter Seeking*—as well as the nonfiction book *Simple Acts of Moving Forward: A Little Book About Getting Unstuck*. She and her husband, Jim, a professional photographer, live in Chicago.

If you are interested in having Vinita facilitate a workshop in your area, you can contact her at

Vinita Hampton Wright
934 S. Eberhart Ave.
Chicago, IL 60619
vinitawright@sbcglobal.net